THE FLASH GORDON SERIALS, 1936-1940

THE FLASH GORDON SERIALS, 1936–1940

A Heavily Illustrated Guide

Roy Kinnard, Tony Crnkovich
and R.J. Vitone

McFarland & Company, Inc., Publishers
Jefferson, North Carolina, and London

ALSO BY ROY KINNARD AND TONY CRNKOVICH

The Films of Fay Wray (2005; paper 2008)

ALSO BY ROY KINNARD

*Science Fiction Serials: A Critical Filmography
of the 31 Hard SF Cliffhangers; With an Appendix
of the 37 Serials with Slight SF Content* (1998; paper 2008)

Horror in Silent Films: A Filmography, 1896–1929 (1995; paper 1999)

*"The Lost World" of Willis O'Brien:
The Original Shooting Script of the 1925 Landmark
Special Effects Dinosaur Film, with Photographs* (1993)

ALL FROM MCFARLAND

Frontispiece: Charles Middleton as Ming the Merciless in *Flash Gordon* (1936).

LIBRARY OF CONGRESS CATALOGUING-IN-PUBLICATION DATA

Kinnard, Roy, 1952–
The Flash Gordon serials, 1936–1940 : a heavily illustrated guide /
Roy Kinnard, Tony Crnkovich and R.J. Vitone.
p.   cm.
Includes index.

ISBN 978-0-7864-3470-1
illustrated case binding : 50# alkaline paper ∞

1. Flash Gordon films — History and criticism.
I. Crnkovich, Tony, 1962–   II. Vitone, R.J.   III. Title.
PN1995.9.F558K56   2008   791.43'75 — dc22   2008006479

British Library cataloguing data are available

On the cover: Poster art for the 1936 serial *Flash Gordon*,
reissued as *Rocket Ship* (Universal Pictures/Photofest)

Manufactured in the United States of America

*McFarland & Company, Inc., Publishers
Box 611, Jefferson, North Carolina 28640
www.mcfarlandpub.com*

To
Jean Rogers
(1916–1991)
in heartfelt remembrance
and appreciation

Acknowledgments

The authors are indebted to the following individuals for their contributions to this book: Buster Crabbe (deceased), for consenting to an extensive telephone interview in 1983; Jean Rogers (deceased), for also consenting to a lengthy phone interview in 1981, and for inviting me into her home in Sherman Oaks, California, on several occasions; Carroll Borland (deceased), who shared her memories by phone in 1985; film historian George Turner (deceased), who shared my interest in these films and encouraged me to write this book; Don Lee and Russ Butner of the Margaret Herrick Library (Academy of Motion Picture Arts and Sciences); Sandy Williamson and Jeff Pirtle of the Universal Studios Archives and Collections, Document Management Division, Universal City, California; Roni Lubliner of NBC-Universal; Ned Comstock of the University of Southern California (Cinema–TV library), Los Angeles; Josie Walters-Johnston, reference librarian (moving image section), Library of Congress, Washington, D.C.; Tom Sand; and Ita Golzman and Frank Caruso of Hearst Entertainment. In reflecting on these acknowledgments, my only true regret is the number of times I have had to type the word "deceased" in this paragraph. May God bless all of the above who are no longer with us. — R.K.

Table of Contents

Preface

Artist/writer Alex Raymond's newspaper comic strip *Flash Gordon* debuted on January 7, 1934, and was an immediate hit with a Depression-era public sorely in need of escapist adventure. Conceived by Raymond and the Hearst newspaper chain as competition for the already-established rival strip *Buck Rogers*, *Flash Gordon* soon eclipsed *Buck* in popularity. Tightly plotted and extremely well drawn, *Flash Gordon* was imbued with swashbuckling romanticism and exotic interplanetary settings that transported world-weary audiences of the time into another, more entertaining world.

The strip quickly became one of those pop-culture sensations that was discussed by readers around thousands of office water-coolers and factory lunch tables the next day. While both *Buck Rogers* and *Flash Gordon* were ostensibly science fiction, it was *Buck Rogers* that emphasized sci-fi gadgetry and jargon, while *Flash Gordon*, with its towering heroes, beautiful women and unspeakably evil villains, was more fantasy-oriented; Raymond's strip had more in common with the worlds of Edgar Rice Burroughs and *The Wizard of Oz* than the largely austere realm of sci-fi.

In the early 1900s, newspaper circulation, particularly in metropolitan areas, drove every facet of a paper's daily operations. Newspaper baron William Randolph Hearst was a canny publisher who recognized the drawing power of colorful, escapist fare. Comic strips, in both daily and Sunday installments, served to lighten the impact of the often grim daily news, and a popular "talked about" comic strip could increase readership. Hearst's King Features Syndicate sought out, developed, and showcased the comic-strip work of many artists. In a few short years, Sunday comics sections grew from simple fillers to enormous inserts, sometimes using as many as three full-color sections. Every type of feature found its way into these garishly-colored pages; humor, soap opera, historical, crime/detective/mystery, fantasy, adventure and military, all scrambled for the readers' attention. Imitation was inevitable; if a particular western feature generated favorable public reaction, several "new" western strips would appear in short order. *Flash Gordon* wasn't a direct copy of *Buck Rogers*, but its creation certainly grew out of that earlier strip's success.

Alex Raymond was a 24-year-old artist who had worked in the newspaper comic strip field as an assistant and "ghost" for other artists. *Flash Gordon* was his personal creation. A Sunday insert-only, full-page feature, the strip chronicled the interplanetary adventures of Flash Gordon, "Yale graduate and world-renowned polo player." In other words, Flash was a "gentleman"—a WASP in good standing; and who better to battle archvillain Ming

Jean Rogers and Buster Crabbe as Dale and Flash.

the Merciless, whose very appearance suggested the oriental and "foreign," thereby playing into the "yellow peril" slant of Hearst's newspapers? King Features snapped it up, and the strip appeared, full-blown and in full color, in early 1934. Drawing at that time in a tight, blocky style, Raymond packed those early pages with an abundance of plot, and introduced a wide array of characters with dizzying speed, but with narrative clarity. Readers knew in no uncertain terms just what was going on, what the dangers were, and who was on whose side.

It's difficult today to even imagine the cultural impact that *Flash Gordon* had on newspaper readers at that time. There had been science-fiction strips before, but Raymond had virtually reinvented the genre. His work on the strip, particularly as he continually developed his art style to fully illustrate his fantastic vision, represents one of the true milestones of the newspaper comics market. Raymond brought a new artistic depth to the "funny pages." After an early period of experimentation with his characters, Raymond launched Flash Gordon and his extended "family"—Dale Arden and Dr. Hans Zarkov—on a series of outer-space adventures that H. G. Wells (and certainly Edgar Rice Burroughs) would have appreciated.

Flash battled monsters and despotic rulers on every corner of the planet Mongo, all of them controlled by Ming the Merciless, supreme dictatorial ruler of Mongo and self-proclaimed Emperor of the Universe. Ming ruled Mongo with sadistic ruthlessness, consolidating his power by pitting the various tribes of the planet against each other, and, in the process, unwittingly uniting them in their hatred of him. Raymond's stunning artwork vividly transported the reader to Mongo's exotic locales, with his style growing and maturing until, by 1937, his work had attained a high level matched by few others in the field. Given free reign over plot, design, and even page layout, he opened up the Sunday comics page in new, visually exciting ways.

Working at times from live models, he captured unique details with an artist's sensitive perception, as though through a camera lens, and Raymond's creation was a natural for the movies. In 1936, Universal Pictures released the first movie based on the property, a 13-chapter weekly serial starring Olympic swimming champion-turned-actor Buster Crabbe in the heroic title role. Certainly one of the best (and most faithful) live-action comic strip adaptations ever produced by Hollywood, *Flash Gordon* (with a credit line unabashedly proclaiming it as "Alex Raymond's cartoon strip" beneath the main title) was an immediate hit, spawning two sequels over the next four years.

These three films went on to retain their popularity in theatrical re-issues, decades-long syndicated television exposure, and now on home video. Over the years, the *Flash Gordon* serials have inspired any number of imitation serials, feature films, and TV shows, as well as certain elements of the George Lucas *Star Wars* movies.

This is the first book-length history of the *Flash Gordon* serials. The authors have arranged the material in a chapter-by-chapter format conforming to the structure of the serials themselves. Included are full cast and credit information, chapter-by-chapter story synopses, and production and technical notes (in the "comments" section following each chapter story synopsis).

Interspersed throughout are direct quotations and comments from Flash Gordon cast members Buster Crabbe, Jean Rogers and Caroll Borland. These quotes are, for the most part, drawn from three main interviews conducted by author Roy Kinnard in 1981 (Jean Rogers), 1983 (Buster Crabbe) and 1985 (Carroll Borland), as well as previous and subsequent conversations with Crabbe and Rogers. These quoted remarks are identified by the bracketed italicized notation "[*Interview*]" after each comment.

Information on shooting schedules, budgets, production costs and salaries are quoted from official Universal Pictures file documents, except in the case of the first serial, *Flash*

Gordon (1936), for which studio records are not available. Access to the extant production records and memos was made possible by Ned Comstock of the University of Southern California's Cinema-TV Library; Don Lee, reference librarian at the Margaret Herrick Library; and Sandy Williamson and Jeff Pirtle of the Universal Studios Archives and Document Management Division, who were extremely helpful in pointing us in the right direction. They all have our sincerest thanks. Original release dates for the serials are taken from contemporaneous issues of *The Motion Picture Herald*, and running times were ascertained by clocking DVDs and/or 16mm prints of the serials.

A History of the Flash Gordon Serials

The theatrical movie serial is a long-defunct and neglected screen format, almost forgotten today, its fading memory kept alive only by a dwindling number of fans and enthusiasts. Drama presented in separate weekly installments now exists only in the form of TV soap operas, its movie equivalent of decades past unknown to a public generally indifferent to classic films. Yet these old serials, three of them in particular — the trilogy of *Flash Gordon* serials, starring Buster Crabbe — have had a continuing influence on modern films, especially the work of George Lucas in his *Star Wars* series. This fact alone would seem to indicate that the best of the serials (and the three *Flash Gordon* productions represent the genre's pinnacle) are at least deserving of serious discussion and preservation. This book is intended as both a history and appreciation of these classic films.

The motion picture serial (aside from a handful of notable foreign efforts, such as director Louis Feuillade's *Les Vampires* [France, 1916], most were produced in America) began in the silent era when a publication called *McClure's Ladies' World*, in conjunction with the Thomas Edison studios, produced, in 12 weekly chapters, a screen version of its serialized story *What Happened to Mary?*, with Mary Fuller in the title role. In a primitive example of media synergy, the screen adaptation was intended to promote the magazine version, and vice versa. This was in 1912, just as movies were beginning to grow and mature as an art form, with longer, more prestigious features created by innovative directors like D. W. Griffith starting to appear. The second movie serial, *The Adventures of Kathlyn*, starring Kathlyn Williams, was released in 12 chapters by Chicago's Selig Polyscope Co. in 1913.

The next year — 1914 — saw the most famous of all silent serials, *The Perils of Pauline*, released by Pathé in 20 chapters. Directed by Louis Gasnier and Donald McKenzie, with Pearl White starring in the title role, this benchmark film laid down the precepts that all serials produced over the next four decades would adhere to, with its resourceful heroine escaping from a contrived peril week after week. Unlike subsequent chapterplays, though, the weekly narratives of *The Perils of Pauline* were largely self-contained and resolved at each chapter's conclusion, rather than abruptly cutting off in "cliffhanger" situations; but the basic form of the movie serial was established with this film. It was produced at a time when the issue of women's rights was at the forefront of public discourse, and audiences readily identified with the fearless and daring Pauline — the serial made Pearl White a star and firmly established a new screen genre.

The silent movie serials continued to grow in appeal throughout the late teens and early twenties, and were dependable money-makers for the studios, playing in 4,000 theaters across the country and helping to generate the regular income needed to keep the production companies solvent. Unlike the later sound serials, the silent chapterplays were accepted by adult filmgoers as a staple of movie programs, while their sound-era counterparts would be relegated almost exclusively to Saturday kids' matinees. Still, the silent serials, audience favorites or not, were, like most "bread and butter" product, hardly respected by studio insiders or serious film critics. As the 1920s progressed and Jazz Age moviegoers became increasingly more sophisticated, the serials began to wane in popularity. By the arrival of sound they had been almost completely marginalized by the film industry. Although a variety of studios and independent companies produced serials during the silent and early sound period, after 1937 chapterplays were made only by Universal, Columbia and Republic. Serials might have vanished entirely by 1935 had it not been for the efforts of one producer, Henry MacRae.

In 1935 Universal Pictures — the studio that had startled the moviegoing public in 1931 with *Dracula* and *Frankenstein*— acquired the film rights to several newspaper comic strips published by King Features Syndicate, including properties like *Secret Agent X-9*, *Ace Drummond*, *Jungle Jim* and *Flash Gordon*, correctly speculating that the established popularity of the strip characters would virtually guarantee the success of any serial based on them. *Tailspin Tommy*, the first serial based on a comic strip, had been profitable for Universal in 1934, prompting a quick sequel, *Tailspin Tommy in the Great Air Mystery*, in 1935. Universal paid $10,000 for the rights to *Flash Gordon* shortly thereafter.

Universal's short subject and serial department was then under the supervision of Canadian-born Henry MacRae (1876–1944), who had started in films with Chicago's Selig Polyscope Co. MacRae, a long-time crony and associate of studio founder Carl Laemmle, had been producing and directing at Universal since 1914, and had been almost single-handedly responsible for bringing serials into the sound era with his ground-breaking 1930 production *The Indians Are Coming*.

The dynamic possibilities of artist/writer Alex Raymond's *Flash Gordon* comic strip, with its rocketships, rayguns, and romantic interplanetary adventures as Flash and his compatriots battled Ming the Merciless for control of the Earth, were obvious, and Universal, at MacRae's urging, took a big chance on the property by investing considerably more money than usual on the project. The average production cost for a serial made by Universal during the 1930s was around $200,000, but the budget necessary to bring the outer space exploits of Flash Gordon to the screen was reportedly $350,000, an amount exceeding that allotted most top-of-the-line features at the time.

Despite this comparatively lavish funding, a lot of economizing was still required. That $350,000 budget, after all, had to be stretched over thirteen 20-minute episodes with a combined running time of over four hours. There was enough money for several expansive (if somewhat empty) sets, such as Ming's throne room, the open areas filled in with draperies and oversized pottery, but many of the serial's other sets and props were borrowed from a variety of Universal features made at the same time. The huge tower set from director James Whale's *Bride of Frankenstein* (1935) appears in chapters 2 and 3. The underground crypt from the same film (minus the dust and cobwebs) was also used as a dungeon in one of the later chapters. The spacious interior of an observatory constructed for

Buster Crabbe as Flash in a publicity pose for *Flash Gordon* (1936).

The Invisible Ray (1936), refitted with futuristic electrical devices, became Ming's laboratory. The crackling, sparkling "mad lab" electrical machines were designed by Kenneth Strickfaden, and were seen in the Universal Frankenstein movies, as well as countless other horror films and serials of the 1930s and '40s. A statue of the Egyptian god Amon-Ra used in the Boris Karloff feature *The Mummy* (1932) represented a deity on the planet Mongo in a couple of scenes; and even Doctor Zarkov's rocketship was a second-hand acquisi-

Buster Crabbe in a tense moment from *Flash Gordon*, chapter 1.

tion — a scale model that had seen previous use in the 1930 Fox feature *Just Imagine*, a loony science-fiction musical that also yielded some impressive outtake footage of a gigantic leering idol used to represent Mongo's "Great God Tao," with the omnipotent deity moving its arms and rolling its eyes as it is worshipped by an energetic, gyrating chorus line of scantily-clad dancing girls. This scene, along with other incidental footage from

Just Imagine, was used to good advantage, helping to provide the necessary "epic" feel. The higher budget also permitted many luxuries usually denied serials, such as glass paintings and some brief split screen shots. *Flash Gordon* still has an inescapably "rough" physical look, but, it should be noted, this does not detract from (and may even add to) the viewer's enjoyment of the movie.

The *Flash Gordon* soundtrack is interesting. A lot of crude overdubbing was used to cover gaps and inconsistencies in the dialogue as originally filmed (shooting was so rushed that the actors sometimes didn't have time to memorize their lines!). Not much care was taken with this dialogue looping; the same voice (supplied by Universal film editor Saul A. Goodkind), for instance, is used over and over. The memorable sound effects have a raw power that enhances the visuals; but of the many creative factors that contribute to the artistic success of this serial and its two sequels, the music is one of the most important elements. The music score for *Flash Gordon* is a veritable crazy quilt blend of scores from other Universal films of the same period, including Heinz Roemheld's music for *White Hell of Pitz Palu* (1930), *The Invisible Man* (1933), *The Black Cat* (1934), and *Bombay Mail* (1934); W. Franke Harling's music for *Destination Unknown* (1933); and Karl Hajos' score for *Werewolf of London* (1935). Not *all* of the score was borrowed—the music for the main and end chapter titles, as well as the mournful, dirge-like theme heard during the printed recap at the beginning of each chapter, was composed specifically for the serial by Clifford Vaughan. This patchwork scoring is surprisingly effective; the music in *Flash Gordon* often works extremely well, improving and elevating scenes that are otherwise weak in content or directorial style. Classical music is also employed; in chapter 1, Richard Wagner's "Good Friday Prelude" from the opera *Parsifal* (used in Harling's *Destination Unknown* score) is used to impressive effect during Zarkov's rocketship flight from Earth to Mongo.

In the second serial, *Flash Gordon's Trip to Mars*, the music score was dominated by Franz Waxman's excellent compositions for *Bride of Frankenstein* (1935). In fact, moviegoers of the era were more familiar with Waxman's music through *Mars* than through *Bride*, which, although now justifiably regarded as a classic, was not a widespread hit on its original 1935 release.

The serial's art director was Ralph Berger, who also designed the 1932 Bela Lugosi thriller *White Zombie*, and the 1935 serial *The Lost City*, which, although a vastly inferior serial, has many visual similarities to *Flash Gordon*. Some of the costumes worn by the actors in *Flash Gordon*, especially the Roman armor of Ming's guards, may appear incongruous, but they are, in fact, perfectly in tune with Alex Raymond's original comic strip drawings; and a few of them, like the costumes worn by Flash, Ming, Prince Barin and Officer Torch, are nearly exact reproductions of Raymond's newsprint originals. No expense was spared on this wardrobe; actress Jean Rogers (Dale Arden) recalled:

> They used to spend *so* much money on clothes, and even though it was in black-and-white, they had to have the colors bright and so forth. Ming's costume was real fur, and that was a red velvet cloak he wore ... and that white dress (if you can *call* it a dress) that I wore, with the gold trim, that was *beautiful* material. They used *very* expensive material for the dresses and things in *Flash Gordon*; they were *very* beautifully-made, and they were made *for* the movie [*Interview*].

Flash (Buster Crabbe) escapes with Dale (Jean Rogers) in chapter 3 of *Flash Gordon*. The set was originally constructed for *Bride of Frankenstein* (1935).

The special effects in *Flash Gordon* may look crude today in our modern age of computer-generated screen fantasies, but taking into account the rushed schedule and high-pressure conditions they worked under, not to mention the lack of interdepartmental studio cooperation (denied to all serials), co-director of photography Jerry Ash, ASC (1892–1953), did a commendable job shooting the scale models and miniature sets. Most of the non-effects scenes were shot by Richard Fryer, ASC (1894–1953).

163-34-EP2

James Pierce as Prince Thun in *Flash Gordon* (1936).

Flash Gordon was quickly filmed on a schedule of only six weeks or so during January and February of 1936, with production wrapping in late February. Denied access to Universal's excellent miniature department (then under the supervision of John P. Fulton, ASC), Ash had to shoot the serial's miniatures quickly, using a warehouse on Universal's backlot German Street (originally constructed for the studio's 1930 epic *All Quiet on the*

The costumes of *Flash Gordon* (1936). Pictured are Richard Alexander, James Pierce and Buster Crabbe in a scene from chapter 13.

Western Front) as a stage. The miniature rocketships in *Flash Gordon*, each about two feet in length, were either manipulated by wires in puppet fashion or suspended in a fixed position in front of a moving background representing passing clouds. These rocketship models, at least nine of which were made (the most shown onscreen in a single shot), were fashioned out of wood (with copper fins and detailing) by propman Elmer A. Johnson, head of the studio's wood and plaster shops. Vital special effects processes, such as rear-screen projection, traveling mattes and stop-motion animation, were not available to Jerry Ash and his crew. Simple split-screen composite photography was used for a brief shot in chapter 1, in which Flash, Dale and Zarkov are attacked by huge dragons as they arrive on Mongo (the monsters were photographically enlarged lizards, "customized" with rubber fins), but almost all of the special effects were achieved cheaply, quickly, and in the camera during filming. Though not convincing in a realistic sense, the special effects possess an almost dreamlike quality, and do work within the self-contained comic strip–inspired world of the serial, a world in which only a handful of shots depicting normal, realistic scenery are allowed to intrude.

Many of the film's best qualities can be attributed to first-time director Frederick Stephani (1903–1962), who was also the chief writer, penning the screenplay with veteran scripters George Plympton, Basil Dickey and Ella O'Neill, never straying far from Raymond's original strip. Related to producer Henry MacRae, experienced serial writer Ella O'Neill had been a practicing attorney in Chicago years before, and was a language specialist.

Stephani, born in Germany, was a political activist in Hungary and had worked in

classical theater; he attained a degree of success as a screenwriter with the arrival of the sound era in Hollywood. In directing *Flash Gordon*, Stephani contributed (when time permitted) some atmospheric staging and dramatic camera angles. The screenplay's bizarre (and almost quasi-religious) "good vs. evil" slant possesses considerable emotional power. Stephani had been under contract to Universal as a writer for several years by this point, and had written one of the early treatments for Tod Browning's *Dracula* in 1930. Buster Crabbe remembered the neophyte director as "capable and in command" [*Interview*], but did not feel that Stephani had the necessary experience of veteran serial directors like Ray Taylor (and Taylor himself was

Jean Rogers as Dale, in a scene from *Flash Gordon*, chapter 5.

brought in to shoot a few scenes [uncredited] in order to bring the film in on schedule). After directing *Flash Gordon*, Stephani left Universal to produce films like *Tarzan's New York Adventure* (1942) for M-G-M, and also wrote a treatment for a proposed sequel to *Casablanca* (1942), which was never produced. He did not return to directing until the 1950s, in TV series like *My Friend Flicka* and *Waterfront*. Compared to other serials, *Flash Gordon* is remarkable because it combines all of its elements — story, acting, music, design and photography — into a solid whole; and there are few movies of any type, from any era, that attain this goal.

Much of the film's enduring charm is due to the chemistry of the actors, principally Buster Crabbe (Flash), Jean Rogers (Dale Arden), Charles Middleton (Ming the Merciless), Priscilla Lawson (Princess Aura) and Frank Shannon (Doctor Zarkov). Oakland, California, native Buster Crabbe (1907–1983), a 1932 Olympic swimming champion, always underrated and surely the most dramatically capable athlete-turned-actor in movies, was perfect as Flash, having won the role over John Hall, who also auditioned (among others). Crabbe, recalling *Flash Gordon*, said:

> To bring it in on schedule, we had to average 85 set-ups a day; that means moving and arranging the heavy equipment we had, the arc lights and everything, 85 times a day. We had to be in make-up every morning at 7:00, and on the set at 8:00 ready to go. They'd knock off for lunch, and then we always worked after dinner; they'd give us a break of a half-hour or 45 minutes and then we'd go back on the set and work until 10:30 every night. It wasn't fun, it was a lot of work! [*Interview*].

Stunningly beautiful young actresses Jean Rogers (1916–1991) and Priscilla Lawson (1914–1958), only 20 and 22 years old, respectively, were ideal as the "good" (Rogers) and "bad" (Lawson) girls. Their vibrant beauty adds a sexual element missing from most serials. Veteran character actor Charles Middleton (1874–1949), whose entertaining, theatrical villainy enlivened several Laurel & Hardy films and many "B" westerns, found the role he was born to play in Ming the Merciless, and the sixty-year-old actor clearly relished the assignment. Jean Rogers recalled of Middleton:

> When he was in his cloak, and made up like Ming, he strutted around like Ming, he really did *strut*! He was a very nice guy, but he had to stay in character. The minute he put on his street clothes, he was a different person ... it was really quite amusing! [*Interview*].

Born into a wealthy Kentucky family, Middleton had entered show business (beginning in carnivals and vaudeville with wife Leora Spellmeyer) to express himself creatively. Arthur Middleton, an original signer of the Declaration of Independence, was an ancestor, and actor Burr Middleton is his grandson. An imposing, severe-looking 6-footer, Middleton had a commanding physical presence and a rich baritone voice, which he put to good use in his nearly 200 films. He was cast as Abraham Lincoln several times, and also played Jefferson Davis (in the 1940 Errol Flynn vehicle *Virginia City*), as well as (very effectively) Satan in the 1930 Technicolor musical short *The Devil's Cabaret*.

Frank Shannon (1874–1959) played the moralistic scientist and father-figure Dr. Zarkov (supposedly Russian, despite Shannon's incongruous Dublin accent), and Richard Alexander (1902–1989) was the stolid Prince Barin, the rightful ruler of Mongo who had been dethroned by the treacherous Ming. A dependable supporting actor, Alexander had given an impressive

Buster Crabbe and Jean Rogers as Flash and Dale.

performance in the prestigious *All Quiet on the Western Front*, and was regularly used in supporting roles by Cecil B. DeMille, appearing in that director's *King of Kings* (1927), *The Sign of the Cross* (1932), *Cleopatra* (1934), *The Plainsman* (1936), and *Union Pacific* (1938).

On its original release, *Flash Gordon* was so successful that it played evening performances at first-run theaters, one of only a handful of sound serials to do so. The industry

trade paper *Variety*, in its March 11, 1936, review, called the 13-chapter epic "An unusu-
ally ambitious effort ... with feature production standards that have been maintained as to
cast, direction and background." The serial proved to be one of Universal's most profitable
1936 releases. Later that year, a re-edited 68-minute feature version of *Flash Gordon* was
released by Universal. The film was an excellent condensation of the serial, with re-scored
music and a re-mixed sound effects track. It was retitled *Rocket Ship* for reissue in 1938.
But before the release of *Flash Gordon*, Universal finally collapsed under the weight of its
own shaky finances in May of 1936, with founding owner Carl Laemmle selling out to a
group of investors for only $5,500,000.

The new studio management, headed by executive vice-president Charles R.
Rogers, with William Koenig serving as general production manager, took control on
April 3, 1936, three days before the release of *Flash Gordon*, and made abrupt changes in
Universal product and personnel. Henry MacRae, though considered somewhat profli-
gate in his methods, was retained by the studio bosses, but was now assigned to produce
only two serials a year instead of the four per year he had formerly supervised — the
other two to be made by a rival production team headed by Ben Koenig (younger
brother of William) and Barney Sarecky. The first Koenig-Sarecky effort, *Ace Drummond*
(featuring *Flash Gordon*'s Jean Rogers), was brought in for a cost of only $125,000,
and had been a moderate success. Universal resolved to make a sequel to *Flash
Gordon*, but it would not be produced by MacRae's unit — and would definitely *not* cost
$350,000.

The 15-chapter sequel to *Flash Gordon*, *Flash Gordon's Trip to Mars*, was released in
March of 1938. Filmed from November 19 to December 24, 1937, *Flash Gordon's Trip to
Mars* was budgeted at $168,700 and was completed at a final cost of $182,000 — about *half*
the original's cost. But it was still an elaborate undertaking for a serial, and is, in some
ways, even more entertaining than its progenitor. Although this entry lacks the overall con-
sistency of the first one, the pacing is generally faster, and its more "modern" look com-
pensates somewhat for the serial's budgetary shortcomings. Some of the best-remembered
visuals from the series — the "light bridge," the martian "stratosleds," and so on — are to
be found in *Trip to Mars*; and while the first serial is certainly better, *Flash Gordon's Trip
to Mars* is the best remembered of the series. This is the serial with the eerie "clay people," who seemed even *more* eerie in the original 1938 release prints, which were struck on
Kodak Sonochrome Verdante color film stock to achieve a vibrant green tonal range. The
cast, with most of the principles from the original (with the notable exception of Priscilla
Lawson) reprising their roles, is once again in top form, with the addition of Beatrice
Roberts, a demurely sexy brunette, as the villainous Azura, Queen of Magic, the ruler of
Mars who assists Charles Middleton's Ming the Merciless in his nefarious efforts to conquer the universe and destroy the Earth. Needless to say, they are unsuccessful. Roberts,
a two-time Miss America Pageant entrant (in 1924 and 1925), had been married for seven
years to *Believe It or Not*'s Robert L. Ripley. She was also reputedly the long-time girl-
friend of M-G-M boss Louis B. Mayer. Despite her prominent role in *Trip to Mars* and
the Universal feature *The Devil's Party*, released the same year, she was soon relegated to
bit parts.

The inclusion of comic actor Donald Kerr (1891–1977) as bumbling newspaper
reporter "Happy" Hapgood added some welcome comedy relief as well. A 68-minute re-cut

Buster Crabbe as Flash.

feature version, titled *Rocket Ship*, was prepared and then shelved by Universal. When the notorious Orson Welles radio adaptation of *War of the Worlds* was broadcast by CBS on October 30, causing a very real panic in some areas, Universal exploited the resulting publicity by hurriedly re-titling *Rocket Ship* as *Mars Attacks the World*. The studio's well-oiled distribution arm had prints ready and available at its film exchanges by November 2, and

Jean Rogers as Dale Arden (posing on a *Flash Gordon* set originally constructed for *Bride of Frankenstein*).

the discarded title *Rocket Ship* was subsequently transferred to *Flash Gordon*, the feature version of the *first* serial. (*Mars Attacks the World* is interesting in that it contains several miniature shots made specifically for the feature version and not used in the serial.)

After producing a 12-chapter *Buck Rogers* serial (again starring Buster Crabbe) in 1939 (see *Appendix I*), Universal made the third and last entry in the *Flash Gordon* series, the 12-chapter *Flash Gordon Conquers the Universe*, released in April of 1940. Filmed in less

Priscilla Lawson as Princess Aura.

than a month, from November 27 to December 22, 1939, the final cost of this serial was only $177,000. Buster Crabbe, Charles Middleton and Frank Shannon returned in their familiar roles, but Carol Hughes replaced Jean Rogers (then under contract to 20th Century–Fox) as Dale, with Shirley Deane and Roland Drew playing Aura and Barin. This film was not as wildly successful with the public as the first two, but is still one of the best

153-32-EP2

Frank Shannon as Dr. Zarkov.

serials of the sound era, benefiting from glistening photography and flamboyant art direction (in keeping with the more polished, sophisticated artwork that had appeared in Raymond's strip by this time). There were plans to film a fourth *Flash Gordon* serial after World War II, and Buster Crabbe recalled being contacted about the proposed film but it never materialized. Universal abandoned serials entirely in 1946, depending on reissues of their older chapterplays to exploit what they correctly saw as a waning market.

Serials continued to be produced, by Columbia and Republic, for another decade. Finally, inevitably, they were killed off by competition from television, with die-hard Columbia releasing the last serial, *Blazing the Overland Trail*, in 1956. It was a feeble, ignominious and almost totally unnoticed last gasp, and the movie serial was relegated to cultural oblivion. Today, the silent serials exist (for the most part) in fragments or rarely seen archival prints. Even that most famous of silent serials, *The Perils of Pauline*, survives today only in the form of a drastically re-cut and abridged 9-chapter foreign version, less than half the length of the 20-chapter original. Most of the sound serials do exist, but are either languishing in studio vaults, unseen by the public, or are generally available only in blurry public-domain video

Buster Crabbe and Jean Rogers in a scene from *Flash Gordon* (1936), chapter 1.

copies of substandard quality. A brief "serial revival" in the mid–1960s, spurred on by the popular *Batman* network TV series, resulted in wider distribution and higher visibility for the Republic serials, but those serials, remembered by a cult following for their technical slickness and precise stuntwork, have always been wildly overpraised by those fans. The Republics lack any emotional depth or real characterization, and, in truth, have never really lasted in the general public's collective memory.

The *Flash Gordon* character has seen other incarnations; besides a radio show (starring Gale Gordon as Flash) that ran from April 27 to October 26 of 1935 (*before* the first serial was made), there was a cheaply-produced, foreign-made TV series starring Steve Holland that appeared in 1954. A multi-million dollar widescreen color remake, produced by Dino De Laurentiis, and starring Sam J. Jones as Flash (with Max Von Sydow as Ming), was released by Universal in 1980, but failed to engage the public or generate any box office.

The original *Flash Gordon* serials, though, have endured and stood the test of time, remaining enjoyable even in today's world of slick, computer-generated movie spectacles, kept alive by almost constant TV exposure since the 1950s, and their current accessibility on DVD. The 1950s television prints substituted the name "*Space Soldiers*" for "*Flash Gordon*" in each serial's title to differentiate the serials from the Steve Holland TV series, and

Priscilla Lawson, Buster Crabbe and Jean Rogers are still in character as they celebrate the last day of filming on *Flash Gordon* in late February 1936. Cinematographer Richard Fryer, A.S.C., is barely visible in the background, between Lawson and Crabbe.

for some reason the extraneous "*Space Soldiers*" name has clung to the series in its subsequent editions, even appearing on the cover art of the currently available DVDs. The 16mm TV prints distributed by A.B.C. Films (and then King Features) from the late 1960s onward contained spoken narration added to the printed recap titles on each chapter; otherwise, the main content of the serials has remained unchanged.

In 1966, new — and longer — feature versions were re-edited from the serials. There are four of these: *Spaceship to the Unknown* (from the first serial), *The Deadly Ray from Mars* (from the second serial), *The Purple Death from Outer Space* and *Perils from the Planet Mongo* (these two re-cut from the third serial). All three serials — and these four feature-length re-cuts — are available on DVD (in excellent quality) from Image Entertainment.

In 1996, *Flash Gordon*, the first serial, was designated a cultural treasure and deservedly included in the National Film Registry. Cut from the same celluloid pattern as *The Thief of Bagdad* (1940) and the original *King Kong* (1933), the Flash Gordon serials offer the rarest and most appealing type of "innocent" screen fantasy; and that, along with all the other factors cited here, is the main reason for their continuing appeal to film buffs. It's a price-less, hard-to-duplicate quality well deserving of preservation for future generations.

One:
Flash Gordon (1936)

Production Credits

Flash Gordon (Universal Pictures) Released April 6, 1936. *Producer*: Henry MacRae, *Director*: Frederick Stephani (*2nd Unit*: Ray Taylor), *Screenplay*: Frederick Stephani, George Plympton, Basil Dickey, Ella O'Neill (based on the King Features newspaper feature written and drawn by Alex Raymond), *Art Director*: Ralph Berger, *Photography*: Jerome Ash, ASC, Richard Fryer, ASC, *Electrical Effects*: Norman Dewes, *Electrical Properties*: Kenneth Strickfaden, Raymond Lindsay, *Special Properties*: Elmer A. Johnson, *Film Editors*: Saul A. Goodkind, Edward Todd, Alvin Todd, Louis Sackin. *Original Music*: Clifford Vaughan, David Klatzkin (music prepared by Jacques Aubran), *Sound System*: RCA, *Running Time*: 245 minutes.

Chapter Titles

(1) "The Planet of Peril," (2) "The Tunnel of Terror," (3) "Captured by Shark Men," (4) "Battling the Sea Beast," (5) "The Destroying Ray," (6) "Flaming Torture," (7) "Shattering Doom," (8) "Tournament of Death," (9) "Fighting the Fire Dragon," (10) "The Unseen Peril," (11) "In the Claws of the Tigron," (12) "Trapped in the Turret," (13) "Rocketing to Earth"

Cast

Larry "Buster" Crabbe (*Flash Gordon*), Jean Rogers (*Dale Arden*), Charles Middleton (*Emperor Ming*), Priscilla Lawson (*Princess Aura*), Frank Shannon (*Doctor Zarkov*), Richard Alexander (*Price Barin*), John Lipson (*King Vultan*), Theodore Lorch/Lon Poff (*High Priest*), James Pierce (*Prince Thun*), Earl Askam (*Officer Torch*), Duke York, Jr. (*King Kala*), Muriel Goodspeed (*Zona*), Richard Tucker (*Professor Gordon*), George Cleveland (*Professor Hensley*), Constantine Romanoff (*ape man*), Bull Montana (*ape man*), Sana Raya (*Tigron mistress*), Lynton Brent (*passenger plane pilot*), House Peters, Jr. (*shark man*), Jerry Frank (*shark man*), Ray "Crash" Corrigan (*orangopoid*), Al Ferguson (*soldier*), Glenn Strange (*soldier/armored guard/cave monster/fire monster*), Carroll Borland (*handmaiden*), Don Brodie (*observatory scientist*), Lane Chandler (*shark man/soldier*), William Desmond (*hawkman "melting ray" commander*), John Bagni (*hawkman "throne room" guard*), Fred Kohler, Jr. (*soldier/armored guard*), George MacGrill (*soldier*), Charles McMurphy (*hawkman "atom furnace" slavedriver*), Olive Hatch (*Aura's handmaiden*), Fred Scott (*soldier with drugged wine*), Fred O. Sommers (*shark man*), Bunny Waters (*shark man*), Charles "Slim" Whitaker (*prison guard*), Harry Wilson (*sentry*), with Jim Corey, Monte Montague, Bob Kortman, Howard Christie.

FEATURE VERSIONS

Flash Gordon (1936), running time 68 minutes (a.k.a. *Rocket Ship*), released theatrically; and *Spaceship to the Unknown* (1966), running time 97 minutes, distributed to television and non–theatrical rental markets.

VIDEO AVAILABILITY

Both the complete serial, *Flash Gordon*, and the feature version, *Spaceship to the Unknown*, have been released on DVD by Image Entertainment. *Rocket Ship* has been released on DVD by Sinister Cinema.

....

Chapter 1: "The Planet of Peril"

Synopsis

An unknown planet, on a collision course with Earth, has disrupted global weather patterns and thrown human civilization into chaos. As doomsday inevitably approaches and riots sweep the globe, the rogue planet is studied by Professor Gordon and his assistant, Professor Hensley, at Dorr Observatory in New York. They come to the grim realization that the world will soon be "smashed to atoms."

Meanwhile, Professor Gordon's son Flash is on his way home aboard a transcontinental passenger flight when the plane is suddenly caught in turbulence caused by the violent storms. Aboard the plane, he meets Dale Arden, a beautiful young girl; and when the plane is thrown out of control by a meteor shower, Flash, Dale and the other passengers are forced to bail out just as the aircraft is destroyed by a meteor.

Parachuting to safety in a remote forest area, Flash and Dale see a futuristic rocketship nearby and are startled when Doctor Zarkov suddenly appears, aiming a gun at them, and declares that the rocketship is his invention and that he intends to make a space flight to the approaching planet in an effort to save the Earth. Believing that the planet is highly radioactive, and that the radioactive power can be harnessed to divert its course from the Earth, he beseeches Flash to help him. Flash agrees, but insists, over Zarkov's objections, that Dale accompany them.

Together, they blast off in Zarkov's rocketship, and after a perilous flight through outer space, with Dale fainting from lack of oxygen and the rocketship passing through "the Death Zone" ("a zone devoid of any force," as Zarkov explains), the craft arrives on the mysterious planet, descending into a craggy, desolate valley and landing safely as Zarkov engages a "counter-magnet" to reduce the ship's terrific speed.

Leaving the rocketship, Flash, Dale and Zarkov are attacked and nearly killed by giant carnivorous reptiles before another rocketship suddenly appears in the skies above and destroys the monsters with a powerful death ray. The alien rocketship lands, and a soldier, accompanied by two armored guards, approaches Flash, Dale and Zarkov, harshly announcing that they are under arrest and are to be taken before Ming, "Emperor of the Universe."

Flash resists their captors, struggling briefly with the guards, but at Zarkov's urging he agrees to board the rocketship and is flown with Dale and Zarkov to a distant

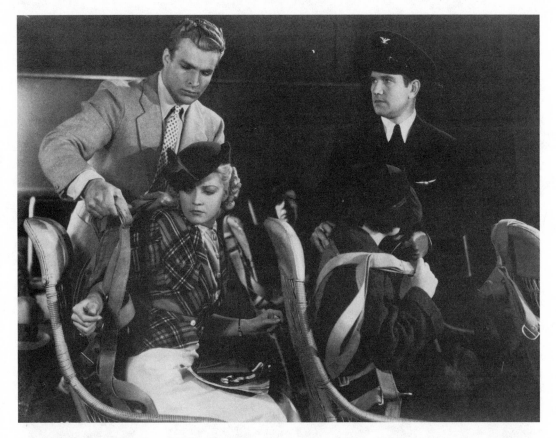

Flash (Buster Crabbe) and Dale (Jean Rogers) prepare to bail out of their doomed passenger plane while the pilot (Lynton Bent) looks on.

mountaintop city, where they are taken to the throne room of Emperor Ming, the cruel tyrant who rules the planet.

In response to Zarkov's concerns about the fate of Earth, Ming declares that he alone controls the course of his own planet, and that there will be no collision with Earth. Ming announces that he will destroy the Earth in his own way, and when Zarkov attempts to dissuade Ming by suggesting that he conquer Earth instead of destroying it, Ming is taken with the idea. Impressed with Zarkov's scientific knowledge, Ming orders the scientist to be imprisoned in his laboratory.

Ming's beautiful daughter, Princess Aura, suddenly appears at the throne and exchanges an icy glare with Dale before noticing Flash, at whom she stares with undisguised lust. Flash ignores Aura and leaps into action when Ming blatantly expresses his interest in Dale, nearly strangling the tyrant. Flash is subdued by Ming's soldiers, and Ming orders Flash thrown into a combat arena where Flash is forced to battle three subhuman ape-men as a horrified Dale watches. Princess Aura, concerned for Flash, enters the arena over Ming's objections and, seizing a raygun from one of Ming's soldiers, defies her own father, declaring that Flash "has earned the right to live!"

Ming orders Flash dropped through a trapdoor into a pit, but Princess Aura shoots the soldier at the control panel before the trapdoor can be activated. The soldier still manages to throw the trapdoor switch as he collapses, though, and as Dale screams help-lessly, Flash and Aura both fall into the arena pit...

Comments

Chapter 1 of *Flash Gordon* is, if not the greatest single serial chapter ever made, then certainly a strong contender for the title, packing what can only be described as an apoc-alyptic chain of events into its tightly-paced 20 minutes.

Some of the serial's finest technical work can be seen in this opening chapter. The beginning observatory scenes are nicely augmented with expansive glass art, as Professor Gordon (Richard Tucker) peers at the onrushing planet through a telescope that also saw service in the Karloff/Lugosi vehicle *The Invisible Ray*, released the same year. Besides the actual miniature of Zarkov's rocketship, re-used from *Just Imagine*, Universal also purchased some footage (outtakes) from the Fox picture of the craft in flight for re-use in the serial. The explosive initial take-off of Zarkov's rocketship from Earth, and a powerful dramatic shot of it speeding away from Earth directly toward the camera, are from the *Just Imag-ine* footage — all other shots of the rocketship were filmed specifically for the serial. News-reel footage represented the global riots.

Dale (Jean Rogers) and Flash (Buster Crabbe) are wary of Dr. Zarkov (Frank Shannon) as he outlines his plan to save the Earth from destruction.

Dr. Zarkov (Frank Shannon, center) is apparently explaining the operation of his rocketship to Dale (Jean Rogers) and Flash (Buster Crabbe) in a scene that was cut from chapter 1 before *Flash Gordon*'s release.

Top: Zarkov (Frank Shannon), Flash (Buster Crabbe) and Dale (Jean Rogers) are greeted by Officer Torch (Earl Askam) and his soldiers, as Torch prepares to take them to Ming, Emperor of the Universe. *Bottom:* Zarkov (Frank Shannon), Flash (Buster Crabbe) and Dale (Jean Rogers) are forced into Ming's rocketship by Officer Torch (center). Note the support bracing of the rocketship mock-up, visible at far left.

Top: Inside Ming's palace, Zarkov, Dale and Flash are brought before the Emperor. The actor seated on the throne is a stand-in and *not* Charles Middleton, who was (according to Jean Rogers) off the set when this photo was taken. *Bottom:* Flash, Dale and Zarkov are introduced to Ming and his daughter Aura. From left to right: Earl Askam, Jean Rogers, Frank Shannon, Charles Middleton, Priscilla Lawson, Buster Crabbe.

Top: Princess Aura (Priscilla Lawson) fires the raygun at Ming's palace guards just before she and Flash (Buster Crabbe) drop through a trap door. *Bottom: Flash Gordon* (1936) — Chapter 1: After landing on Mongo, Flash and Dale are attacked by giant reptiles.

An impressively-rendered backdrop painting of Ming's mountaintop city (which, judging from the onscreen evidence must be at least 15 by 20 feet in size) is blended into three-dimensional scale model foreground scenery as Zarkov's rocketship lands on Mongo; this same backdrop (or at least footage shot of it for the first serial) was re-used numerous times in all three serials.

The enlarged lizards used to represent giant monsters are combined with the live actors, to demonstrate scale, in some brief shots using simple split-screen composites; the "lizard" technique would be used to a greater extent (and with considerably more finesse) four years later in producer Hal Roach's feature *One Million B.C.*, in which normal reptiles, with rubber horns and fins attached, were used as stand-ins for prehistoric animals.

Two of the three "ape-men" battling Flash in Ming's arena made other film appearances: Bull Montana had played a prehistoric subhuman in *The Lost World* (First National, 1925), and Constantine Romanoff played threatening supporting roles in several films of the era, including *The Affairs of Cellini* (20th Century, 1934). Buster Crabbe recalled shooting the arena fight:

> That was a funny thing.... It was a hard place to fight, no furniture to jump over, no walls to climb or anything. They let these three wild men out, and they had fangs and everything. It

Flash battles Ming's subhuman ape-men in the palace arena. From left: Constantine Romanoff, Buster Crabbe, Bull Montana.

Princess Aura intercedes as Flash defeats the ape-men and is attacked by Ming's soldiers. From left: Buster Crabbe (center), Earl Askam, Priscilla Lawson and (on floor) Constantine Romanoff.

took a day and a half to get this scene, because we had to rehearse, and I had to get rid of one guy before the other guy hit me and so on, and we'd make mistakes and have to repeat. Well, the second afternoon there was just one more guy to throw and I thought, "Well, we finally got it in the can at last," when all of a sudden one of the wild men stood up and said, "Cut, cut!" and Stephani came out of his chair like he was shot out of a cannon, saying, "What the hell's the matter?" And the actor says, "Mr. Stephani, I'm sorry, but I lost my fangs!" It really didn't matter. He could have finished the scene without them, turned his back to the camera or something, but we had to go around and look for the fangs, and we finally found them and completed the scene. It was an exciting scene, a good way to start the serial off [*Interview*].

Crabbe recalled how he was cast in what would be his most famous role:

I got interested in the thing through the Alex Raymond comic strip. When I went home in the evening I'd pick up the paper and find out what old Flash had gotten himself into with Ming or whatever. Inadvertently, back in 1935, I picked up a copy of *The Hollywood Reporter*, and noticed a blurb at the bottom of the page announcing that Universal Studios was going to do a serial of Alex Raymond's comic strip, and in those days I thought, "It's just too fantastic." It was just too crazy to be doing, having these three people get in a rocketship and going off to

Mongo and getting involved in all sorts of things. The announcement also said that if you wanted to try out for the part, to check into the Universal casting office, and if they thought you were likely, they would have a test the following week.

Now, I had done a couple of things at Universal, and the people at the casting office knew me, so I called up a man there by the name of Miller, and told him I'd read the announcement in *The Hollywood Reporter*, and he said, "Do you want to test for the part, Buster?" And I said, "Hell no — but I would like to get on the set and see who's crazy enough to try out for this thing." So he said, "Well, come on out, and I'll get you on the set."

So I went out to the studio the next day, it was a Wednesday or a Thursday. In those days they had just 12 shooting stages at Universal, and they have about 42 now. They told me they were testing on stage 7 or 8, and I wandered on out there and stood off to the side. There were fifteen or sixteen actors there testing, two I noticed right away who I thought were possibilities, and the others I thought didn't qualify. One of the guys that I thought had a chance was an actor by the name of George Bergaman, a nice-looking young man who was into body building and that kind of thing. He was a bit actor in Hollywood, and I had been in a couple of films he'd worked on. I thought he'd be perfect for the part, they'd just have to bleach his hair. The other guy, it was lucky for him that he didn't get the part, because a couple of months later John Ford picked him to play the juvenile lead in a picture he was going to do called *Hurricane*. The actor's name, of course, was Jon Hall, and *Hurricane* made him a star.

Somebody on the set pointed me out to the producer, Henry MacRae, and I found out later

Flash fights for his life against Ming's soldiers as Princess Aura watches anxiously. From left: Priscilla Lawson, Al Ferguson, Buster Crabbe, Earl Askam.

Princess Aura (Priscilla Lawson) defends Flash (Buster Crabbe) with a raygun.

he'd been producing serials at Universal for years. He came over and introduced himself, and asked me, naturally, why I was there. I explained that it was just curiosity on my part, so we talked a little while, and he said, "Well, how would you like to do the part?" And I said, "I really don't know."

So we talked a little further, and he finally said, "You have the part if you want it." And I started to tell him that I was under contract with another studio when he said, "I know, Buster, you're under contract to Paramount ... we'll borrow you." My automatic answer was, "Well, if I'm borrowed, then I'll have to do what the bosses at Paramount tell me to do." But privately I was thinking, "I hope the studio tells them I'm not available." So I shook hands with MacRae and turned to go. I think you know the rest of the story ... [*Interview*].

Flash Gordon's father, in the opening scene, was portrayed by veteran character actor Richard Tucker (1884–1942), who was the first official member of the Screen Actors Guild and a founding member of SAG's board of directors. Professor Gordon's assistant, Professor Hensley, was played by George Cleveland (1885–1957), who, toward the end of his long career, was familiar to TV viewers as "Gramps" on the popular TV series *Lassie*, which ran from 1954 to 1957. Cleveland appeared in 55 episodes.

Jean Rogers and Priscilla Lawson (both of them beauty pageant winners) had been signed by Universal the previous year, and were cast by MacRae from the stable of available contract talent. Lawson had also been a model. According to Jean Rogers, a bit of unexpected re-shooting was mandated when Lawson's ample bosom caught the eyes of

*Top: **Flash Gordon** (1936)—Chapter 1: Ming (Charles Middleton) and his daughter Aura (Priscilla Lawson), accompanied by two of Ming's women, watch as Flash battles the ape-men. The actress in the rear is Carroll Borland (**Mark of the Vampire**). **Bottom:** Dale, horrified, is forced to watch as Flash fights the ape-men in chapter 1 of **Flash Gordon**. From left: Jean Rogers, Charles Middleton, Priscilla Lawson, Earl Askam, Carroll Borland.*

watchful censors; several of her shots were ordered redone, much to producer MacRae's chagrin. Lawson was re-filmed, with restraining bands of cloth placed under her costume [*Interview*]. A couple of the more expensive shots (such as a special effects optical of her firing a raygun) could not be redone, and sharp-eyed viewers can still glimpse the Lawson anatomy in all of its unfettered glory. The actress was also required to do some vocal overdubbing of her dialogue in the arena fight scene; apparently it was decided that a couple of her lines needed more dramatic emphasis, and she looped those portions of her dialogue. This is revealed when the original audio is used at the beginning of the recap footage opening chapter 2.

Another lovely young actress more or less consigned to background action in the serial is Carroll Borland (1914–1994), who the previous year had played Bela Lugosi's vampiric daughter in the M-G-M horror film *Mark of the Vampire*. Borland recalled that she worked on *Flash Gordon* for one (very long) day's shooting (she can be glimpsed in chapters 1, 2, 3, and some later episodes), and that she remembered Buster Crabbe complaining very bitterly about being required to bleach his hair for his role, an observation verified by Crabbe himself, as well as Jean Rogers [*Interview*].

The rocky area where Flash, Dale and Zarkov first land on Mongo and encounter the giant reptiles before they are taken to Ming's palace was an exterior set on the Universal

Flash (Buster Crabbe) assists Dale (Jean Rogers), who has fainted.

backlot. The rock formations were man-made, constructed of hydracal, and the set was originally built for the 1933 Universal feature *Nagana*, directed by Ernest L. Frank. It was re-used countless times in various serials and low-budget westerns.

Out-going studio head Carl Laemmle, Sr. accurately remarked of *Flash Gordon*, while it was in production, "Financially, it is the biggest serial investment ever made."

Trivia Note: Curiously, Ming's planet of Mongo is neither identified nor called by that name for the first time until later in the serial, in chapter 5!

....

Chapter 2: "The Tunnel of Terror"

Synopsis

As Flash and Aura fall into the pit toward certain death, Ming orders a mechanized safety net activated to save his daughter, and the net unfurls across the pit, catching Flash and Aura, and saving them from the carnivorous "dragon of death" waiting in the caverns below. The lecherous Ming orders Dale taken away to be prepared for marriage to him. Aura takes Flash through a secret door in the side of the pit, leading to the caverns below Ming's palace. There they hide from Ming's soldiers, who are searching for them.

After Flash and Aura vanish through a trap door in the arena, Dale (Jean Rogers) is held captive by Ming (Charles Middleton), who makes his carnal desires known.

Princess Aura (Priscilla Lawson) leaves Flash (Buster Crabbe) near one of Ming's rocketships.

Meanwhile, Zarkov, held prisoner in the palace laboratory, is visited by Ming, who declares that he intends to conquer the universe—with Zarkov's assistance. Ming's high priest arrives and is ordered by Ming to prepare Dale for the marriage ceremony by subjugating her will with the "dehumanizer." "Science can conquer all things," he tells Zarkov, "even the human emotions."

In the caverns below the palace, Aura expresses her love for Flash, and then leads him to one of Ming's rocketships at the cavern opening, asking that he remain there until she returns. After she leaves, Flash discards his clothes, shredded in the arena fight, and changes into a uniform he finds aboard the rocketship. When he sees a fleet of circular gyroships flying toward Ming's palace, he fears that Dale and Zarkov will be endangered by the attack. Taking off in the rocketship, Flash engages the gyroships in an air battle and blasts most of them out of the sky. During the course of battle, Flash's rocketship collides with the lead gyroship, and, locked together, they plummet downward, crashing into the rocky valley below.

Flash staggers from the wreckage, only to be confronted by his opponent, Thun, King of the Lion Men, who has also survived the crash. Thun draws his sword and they begin to fight, but Flash wins. When Flash refuses to slay the defeated lion man, Thun learns they are both enemies of Ming, and eagerly joins forces with Flash.

Princess Aura, having returned to the palace after leaving Flash, defiantly intercedes with her father in an attempt to spare Flash's life. As Dale is subjected to the mind-controlling rays of the dehumanizer, Flash and Thun secretly enter the palace laboratory and are told by Zarkov that Mongo will not collide with Earth after all. They also learn that the hypnotized Dale is about to become Ming's unwilling bride.

Flash and Thun try to reach the wedding ceremony through the caverns below Ming's palace but are confronted by Ming's soldiers. As Thun holds them off, Flash continues on; but before he can reach the wedding ceremony and save Dale, he is attacked by a giant monster with lobster-like claws. The beast ensnares Flash in its clutches and slowly crushes him in its overpowering grip...

Comments

The rocketship/gyroship battle that provides a mid-point highlight in chapter 2 uses an impressive number of miniature rocketships manipulated against a huge painted cloudscape. The use of miniatures is obvious to the modern viewer, but the scope of the scene is awesome by serial standards. Buster Crabbe recalled actually seeing some of these scale-

In the caverns below Ming's palace, Princess Aura (Priscilla Lawson) overtly displays her lust for Flash (Buster Crabbe).

Flash (Buster Crabbe) and Thun (James Pierce) hurry to prevent Dale's forced marriage to Ming in chapter 2 of *Flash Gordon*.

model rocketship scenes being shot by Jerry Ash's crew. Crabbe, after reading the description of a miniature scene in the script, had asked Henry MacRae, out of curiosity, how the scenes were being done, and MacRae directed him to the warehouse on Universal's German Street.

There Crabbe recalled seeing Ash and his effects crew filming the miniature rocketships against painted backdrops of cloud scenery, while the wired ships were suspended from microphone booms [*Interview*].

The other memorable scene in chapter 2 is Flash's subterranean encounter with the clawed monster, which borders on the horrific. This lobster-clawed beast is similar to a monster called a "Gocko" in Raymond's comic strip, although it is never referred to as such in the serial. The monster is a costumed actor, Glenn Strange (1899–1973), who later played the Frankenstein Monster in three 1940s Universal films, *House of Frankenstein* (1944), *House of Dracula* (1945) and *Abbott and Costello Meet Frankenstein* (1948). With the costume operated by both Strange inside and exterior wire rigging, the sequence was filmed in a cave at Bronson Canyon, and the filmmakers made clever use of a certain area that offered a false perspective, which made the beast look even larger in relation to Buster

Crabbe. For a couple of shots, a *child*, wearing a miniature Flash Gordon costume, was substituted for Crabbe, further enhancing the illusion. Full of shadowy, atmospheric lighting, this is an impressive scene, and the beast itself prefigures the later rubber-suited giant monsters of the Japanese *Godzilla* films.

James Pierce (1900–1983), who played Thun, had played Edgar Rice Burroughs'

Zarkov (Frank Shannon) is held captive by Ming (Charles Middleton) in the palace laboratory.

Tarzan in *Tarzan and the Golden Lion* (1927), and, although he considered the role detrimental to his career, went on to play the character in 364 15-minute episodes of the Tarzan radio series from 1932 to 1934. Pierce also married Burrough's daughter. Buster Crabbe himself had also played Tarzan, in the 1933 Principal Pictures serial *Tarzan the Fearless*.

There is a nice bit of interplay between Crabbe and Pierce in this episode that demonstrates the extra care that went into this serial. After Flash and Thun initially fight and then realize that they are opposing a common enemy in Ming, Flash offers his hand in friendship. Thun stares blankly for a moment. Being the product of an alien culture, he does not know what a handshake is. Flash notices this, and demonstrates the Earth custom by responding with an energetic handclasp. It's a minor bit, but warmly done and nicely underplayed, adding a bit of characterization to the scene.

Lon Poff (1870–1952), who played Ming's dour high priest in chapters 1 through 3, was dropped from the serial and replaced in later chapters by Theodore Lorch (1873–1947), whose flamboyant theatricality was more appropriate to the role and matched Charles Middleton's similar histrionics nicely. Lorch, who appeared in many films of the period, can also be seen in the Columbia Pictures Three Stooges shorts *We Want Our Mummy* (1939), *Half Wits' Holiday* (1947) and *Hot Scots* (1948). The substitution of Lorch for Poff was smoothly done and barely noticeable, since there were several chapters between in which the high priest character did not appear.

....

Chapter 3: "Captured by Shark Men"

Synopsis

As Flash struggles in the overpowering grip of the cave monster, Thun defeats the last of Ming's soldiers, and, arriving just in time, saves Flash by killing the monster with a raygun. Flash and Thun continue on, arriving at the wedding ceremony as it is in progress. Flash disrupts the proceedings by toppling a huge idol in the midst of the assemblage. Grabbing the hypnotized Dale, he carries her away as Thun holds off Ming and his soldiers with the raygun, before following Flash. The enraged Ming orders one of his men to activate a "water trap," which will "deliver them to Kala, King of the Shark Men."

As they carry Dale to safety, Flash and Thun are attacked by more of Ming's troops. While they fight the soldiers, Dale begins to regain consciousness. Flash takes her away, and Thun stays to fight the remaining soldiers. As Flash and Dale try to find their way out of the palace, Ming, who is secretly watching them through a viewer, activates his water trap.

Flash and Dale suddenly drop through a trapdoor, plunging into a huge water tank, where they are attacked and overpowered by shark men. The shark men take them to a submarine craft, a hydrocycle, and tell them they are to be taken to Kala, king of the shark men. Meanwhile, Princess Aura has left the wedding ceremony and discovered Thun, barely conscious after his fight with Ming's soldiers. She tells him that Flash and Dale have been abducted by the shark men and are being taken to Kala, and that she can enter Kala's palace to rescue them, with Thun's help. Although wary of the duplicitous Aura, Thun agrees.

Flash interrupts Dale's marriage to Ming in *Flash Gordon*, chapter 3. From left: Frank Shannon, Buster Crabbe, Jean Rogers, Charles Middleton, Carroll Borland (in background), Lon Poff.

Aboard the hydrocycle, Flash and Dale are transported to the undersea kingdom of the shark men. After witnessing a savage battle to the death between giant sea monsters, the couple are taken before Kala. Flash defies Kala, a minor despot who rules in Ming's service, openly expressing contempt for him. The angered Kala challenges Flash to a fight, but Flash easily defeats him in hand-to-hand combat. Kala gives Flash his freedom, and has Flash and Dale taken to separate quarters. But Flash, accompanied by guards, is overpowered by the shark men and imprisoned in a huge water tank.

Suspicious of Kala, Dale spies on him and overhears Kala, who has contacted Ming on a "spaceograph," inform the Emperor that Dale will soon be returned to him, and that Flash Gordon will "not trouble you again." Shocked, Dale rushes to Kala's side. "What are you doing to Flash?" she demands. Kala takes Dale to a nearby porthole. Kala forces the horrified girl to watch as Flash's tankroom prison rapidly fills with seawater. Kala unleashes a huge, tentacled "octosac," which ensnares the struggling Flash in its grasp. As Dale screams in horror, Kala declares, "No man can pit his strength against Kala and live..."

Top: Dale (Jean Rogers) and Flash (Buster Crabbe) are taken to the undersea kingdom of the shark men. *Bottom:* Dale (Jean Rogers) is threatened by Kala (Duke York, Jr.), king of the shark men, in a scene from chapter 3 of *Flash Gordon.*

Comments

The plotline of chapters 3 and 4 diverges somewhat from the main narrative of the serial, and this "shark man" material was probably shoehorned into the script because it had been part of the comic strip. Significantly, chapters 3 and 4 were completely eliminated from both of the later feature versions derived from this serial.

At one point in chapter 3, documentary footage of a shark and octopus fighting is used to (rather unconvincingly) depict battling sea beasts; this exact same footage was later utilized by stop-motion animator Ray Harryhausen in his 1953 film *The Beast from 20,000 Fathoms*, with the title monster animated in front of the footage and made to appear as though it devoured the animals!

Duke York, Jr. (1908–1952), cast as King Kala, made a long career out of playing thugs in minor supporting roles. His first documented film appearance was as one of the beast men in *Island of Lost Souls* (Paramount, 1933), and he also appeared in the Three Stooges shorts *Nutty but Nice* (1940) and *Idle Roomers* (1944). In *Idle Roomers* York played a werewolf terrorizing the hapless Stooges. King Kala in *Flash Gordon* was his most prominent role. York died in 1952, committing suicide by shooting himself.

Flash and Thun battle Ming's soldiers as Dale and Aura watch. From left: Buster Crabbe, James Pierce, Jean Rogers, Priscilla Lawson.

The visual quality of the underwater scenes depicting the abduction of Flash and Dale by Kala's shark men was compromised somewhat — much to director Stephani's regret — by the dirtiness of the water, which made the scene look "smoky" on film. Stephani was denied permission to drain and refill the tank with clean water, which would have taken a considerable amount of time. The scene was shot through the window of a round tank on the Universal backlot, and the actors spent the better part of a day in water that was cold as well as dirty. Both Buster Crabbe and Jean Rogers remembered the scene with distaste [*Interview*].

The "octosac" that attacks Flash in Kala's water tank was a rubber prop originally created for an uncompleted 1932 Universal feature, *Black Pearl*. Footage of a live octopus is briefly intercut; and (in an attempt to bring the prop to life) some shots of Crabbe's interaction with the rubber monstrosity were shot in reverse. Crabbe and the octosac were shot "dry" and filmed through a small water-filled aquarium tank, with the actor suspended on a wire as he tried to "swim" away from the monster. Curiously, a brief amount of footage showing the rubber octosac alone turns up in the 1952 feature *The Incredible Petrified World*.

Buster Crabbe (real name Clarence Linden Crabbe) was billed as "Larry 'Buster' Crabbe" by his home studio, Paramount, but was billed simply as "Buster Crabbe" in the main titles of *Flash Gordon* chapters 1 and 2, along with Jean Rogers and Priscilla Lawson (in that order). Beginning with chapter 3, Crabbe's billing was changed to "Larry 'Buster' Crabbe" (probably at Paramount's insistence), and Charles Middleton was given main title billing for the first time, behind Priscilla Lawson.

....

Chapter 4: "Battling the Sea Beast"

Synopsis

As Flash struggles for his life against the octosac, Dale, horrified, turns away, but Kala orders his assistant Zona to force her to watch. Dale faints and is carried away to her quarters by Zona and a shark man. As Flash continues to fight the octosac, Aura and Thun arrive in the undersea throne room. Aura, holding a raygun on Kala, forces Kala to save Flash by draining the water tank. As the tank drains and Flash escapes from the weakened octosac, Kala gives Zona a key and tells her to take Aura to the tankroom door. Thun remains to guard Kala with the raygun.

As Dale revives in her quarters and rejoins Thun and Kala, Aura realizes that Zona is not leading her to the tankroom and struggles with Zona for possession of the key. Finally getting the key from Zona, Aura releases Flash from the tankroom while Dale, Thun and Kala watch through the throne room porthole. Aura then lies to Flash, telling him that Thun has taken Dale back to the surface, with the intention of leading Flash away with her.

Meanwhile, in Ming's laboratory, Zarkov is secretly trying to contact the Earth. On Earth, faint, unidentified signals are received by Professor Gordon, who tells his colleagues that he believes they may emanate from the mysterious planet. Ming suddenly arrives in the laboratory, and, to avoid discovery, Zarkov hurriedly breaks off contact with the Earth.

Dale and Aura watch in horror as Flash, trapped in a water tank, is attacked by an octosac. From left: Jean Rogers, James Pierce, Priscilla Lawson, Duke York, Jr.

Zarkov asks Ming about the fate of his friends, and is told they are being cared for by Kala in his undersea domain. Ming informs Zarkov that Kala is under his total domination, and that the underwater city is protected from the water pressure by a magnetic force controlled from Ming's own laboratory. Officer Torch, Ming's lieutenant, sees a battle between Ming's soldiers and "Queen Mura's tradesmen" on a nearby spaceograph screen, but when he tries to inform Ming, finds him in deep conversation with Zarkov about a new power source that Zarkov has discovered, and is rebuffed by Ming.

Back in Kala's palace, Aura talks Flash into overpowering a shark man guard near a control panel, convincing Flash that it is necessary to aid in their escape. As Flash struggles with the guard, the shark man drops a raygun, and Aura picks it up and fires at the control panel. The panel explodes, and the magnetic force that maintains Kala's palace begins to weaken. When Flash sees this, he no longer believes Aura, and tells her that he is returning to search for Dale. Aura follows him.

As Dale and Thun continue to hold Kala off with the raygun, the air in Kala's palace begins to fade, and Dale loses consciousness. Kala realizes the magnetic power necessary to his city's very existence is failing, and desperately tries to contact Ming on the spaceograph for assistance. In Ming's laboratory, Officer Torch has seen on the spaceograph that

Princess Aura (Priscilla Lawson) frees Flash (Buster Crabbe) from Kala's water tank.

Top: Kala's undersea palace begins to weaken and collapse. From left: Priscilla Lawson, Jean Rogers, Buster Crabbe, James Pierce, Duke York, Jr. *Bottom:* In Ming's laboratory, Zarkov demonstrates a new ray that he has discovered. Pictured are Frank Shannon (left) and Charles Middleton.

Kala's palace has begun to weaken and crumble, and informs Ming. He is too late, though, and as Flash and Aura rejoin Dale, Thun and Kala, tons of seawater destroy the palace walls and crash into the throne room...

Comments

Muriel Goodspeed, who played Kala's curvaceous assistant Zona, was an 18-year-old beauty contest winner from Salt Lake City, Utah. Her only other film credits are appearances in *Bitter Sweet* (1940) and *I Married an Angel* (1942). She was also a vocal stand-in in *Presenting Lily Mars* (1943).

The frequent vocal overdubbing previously mentioned reaches its most obvious and unconvincing level in chapter 4. When an anxious Zarkov asks Ming about Flash and Dale, Ming replies, "Do not worry, your friends are being cared for." The editors then cut to a reaction shot of Zarkov as the off-screen voice (intended to be, but obviously *not*, Charles Middleton's) adds, "By Kala, King of the Shark Men!"

As Kala's palace collapses under the force of water pressure, a scene of mine timbers crumbling amidst inrushing floodwaters is shown. This is stock footage from a 1927 Universal film called *Perch of the Devil*, starring Mae Busch.

When the seawater crashes through the walls of Kala's palace, hundreds of gallons of water were released onto the set through a dump chute, with well-disguised stunt doubles standing in for the actors.

....

Chapter 5: "The Destroying Ray"

Synopsis

As the seawater crashes into Kala's shark palace, Ming uses a ray machine in his laboratory to counteract the magnetic force keeping Kala's city submerged, and the shark palace begins to rise above the water line. Flash, Dale, Aura and Thun leave Kala and his people behind and prepare to leave the shark palace. Aura tries to convince them to return to her father Ming's kingdom, but Thun advises that they go to his father, King of the Lion Men. As they leave, Officer Torch leads a search party, sent by Ming, to retrieve the Earth people and bring them back to his palace.

In Ming's laboratory, Zarkov is visited by Prince Barin, who has stealthily entered Ming's palace. Barin informs Zarkov that he is the rightful ruler of Mongo and had been dethroned as a child by Ming, who murdered Barin's father. Zarkov and Barin form an alliance, and Barin offers to save Zarkov's friends. They leave in Barin's rocketship, flying over a desolate valley as giant carnivorous reptiles watch from below.

Emerging from a cavern as they flee Kala's flood-ravaged kingdom, Flash, Dale, Aura and Thun see King Vultan's hawkmen flying in the sky above them. Aura tells them that King Vultan is an ally of her father. The hawkmen land, attacking them with spears; and as Flash resists them, Thun takes Dale and Aura away to safety. Thun is ambushed and knocked unconscious by the hawkmen. He and Dale are abducted and taken away into the sky, leaving Aura behind.

Top: Flash (Buster Crabbe) fights the hawkmen as Dale (Jean Rogers), Thun (James Pierce) and Aura (Priscilla Lawson) watch. *Bottom:* After Dale and Thun have been abducted by the hawkmen, Prince Barin arrives with Doctor Zarkov. From left: Richard Alexander, Buster Crabbe, Priscilla Lawson, Frank Shannon.

Aura rejoins Flash, who has beaten off the remaining hawkmen, as Barin and Zarkov arrive, landing in Barin's rocketship. Zarkov introduces Barin to Flash, and Barin offers to take Flash to King Vultan's city, which is suspended high in the clouds on gravity-resisting light rays. Flash, Barin, Zarkov and Aura board the rocketship in an attempt to save Dale and Thun.

In Vultan's sky city, the obese, debauched monarch enters his throne room just as an unconscious Dale is being subjected to electronic rays and revived by hawkmen. The captured Thun has been imprisoned in Vultan's atom furnace room, where he and others are whipped by hawkman guards and forced to shovel radium into the atom furnaces in order to power the city's anti-gravity beams.

As Barin's rocketship flies near Vultan's city, it is spotted by hawkmen lookouts, who report this to Vultan. Vultan orders them to destroy the approaching ship with a powerful "melting ray." Dale revives, and as Vultan terrorizes her in his throne room, releasing a zebra-striped bear to frighten the girl, the hawkmen aim their melting ray at Barin's approaching rocketship.

Vultan, continuing his pursuit of Dale, finally sends the pet bear away and approaches Dale with lecherous intent. Although Barin's rocketship is shielded by "resistoforce," the powerful melting ray eventually overcomes the resistoforce, and the ship is rocked by an explosion, hurtling toward the ground far below...

Barin's rocketship is struck by King Vultan's melting ray. From left: Richard Alexander, Buster Crabbe, Priscilla Lawson.

Flash (Buster Crabbe) and Aura (Priscilla Lawson) aboard Prince Barin's rocketship.

Buster Crabbe in a publicity pose with assorted hawkmen.

Comments

The serial's narrative picks up speed and is revitalized with new energy in chapter 5, which contains some of the film's greatest visuals and setpieces.

The furnace room of King Vultan's sky city is an impressive bit of construction, with vertically-operating furnace doors and huge plumes of flame erupting through the openings as the radium is shoveled in. Buster Crabbe recalled in an interview with author Kinnard that the flames were produced by a regulated supply of gas flowing through pipes behind the doors, and that he and the other actors in the scene "didn't have to do much acting" when they reacted to the heat.

Several physically thin, almost emaciated actors were included in this scene, implying that some of the atom-furnace slaves were being physically decimated by the radium they handled. One device in the scene is of particular interest — a huge prop clock-like dial, with a hawkman periodically turning the hands of the device to open and close the furnace doors. This is virtually identical to a similar prop seen in director Fritz Lang's 1926 German-made sci-fi epic *Metropolis*, demonstrating that the designers of *Flash Gordon* had done some extensive research and studied their film history before production began! The "melting ray" manned by Vultan's hawkmen had seen previous use; it was the "moon ray" from Universal's *Werewolf of London* (1935).

Top: Dale (Jean Rogers) is terrorized by King Vultan (John Lipson) in Vultan's sky city. *Bottom:* Aura (Priscilla Lawson) and Dale (Jean Rogers) are protected by Thun (James Pierce) as Flash fights the hawkmen in chapter 5 of *Flash Gordon.*

The fairy-tale image of a city floating in the clouds (Elmer A. Johnson and crew outdid themselves on the miniature for this) was borrowed by George Lucas for his *Star Wars* sequel *The Empire Strikes Back* (1980).

John "Tiny" Lipson (1901–1947), who played the rotund King Vultan, had his most prominent role in this serial. Familiar in numerous bit parts, Lipson can also be seen in Three Stooges shorts, among them *Three Little Pigskins* (1934) and *Dizzy Doctors* (1936).

The sexually-charged scene in which Lipson approaches Jean Rogers — flattened against a wall as she recoils, with her anatomy prominently displayed — was strong stuff at the time, especially for a serial.

The sequence involving Vultan's pet bear, "Urso" (a normal bear made-up with white zebra stripes to make it seem more alien and exotic), was not without difficulties. As Jean Rogers recalled:

> Before we did the scene, there was this horrible commotion in back of the scenery, and we all wondered what in the world it was. The poor bear had been there for just hours and hours waiting to do his scene, and apparently he was not very happy about the whole thing, and he became very ugly with his trainer. So then they said, "Now he's going to chase you across the set," and I was really scared to death because he had just tried to attack his trainer! I *wasn't* very happy about doing that scene! [*Interview*].

· ·

Chapter 6: "Flaming Torture"

Synopsis

As Barin's disabled rocketship plummets toward certain destruction, the ship falls into the gravity-defying rays supporting the sky city. Its descent checked by the rays, the rocketship is held aloft, suspended in mid-air but at Vultan's mercy.

Meanwhile, Vultan's unwanted advances are rebuffed by Dale, who struggles with him until they are interrupted by guards, who bring Flash, Barin, Zarkov and Aura into the throne room. Vultan informs them that they are all his prisoners, and Aura, who openly defies him, is curtly dismissed when she threatens retaliation by her father. Flash and Barin are consigned to the atom furnaces, and Zarkov is sent to Vultan's laboratory.

At Ming's palace, the Emperor is informed by Officer Torch (who had led a group of soldiers in search of the Earth people) that Flash, Dale, Barin, Thun and Aura have all been captured by the hawkmen and taken to Vultan's sky city. Ming, angry at the presumptuous Vultan, makes plans to visit the sky city, reclaim Dale as his intended bride, and reassert his authority over Vultan.

As Flash, Barin and Thun are whipped by the slavedrivers in Vultan's atom furnace, Vultan confronts Zarkov in the laboratory and explains how his city is suspended in the sky by the anti-gravity beams produced in the atom furnace. Soon the supply of radium will be exhausted, he explains, and it will be Zarkov's imposed task to find an alternate energy source — otherwise Flash, Barin and Thun will continue to feed the furnace until they die of radium poisoning.

Aura convinces Dale that Flash's survival depends on Dale giving him up and

Flash (Buster Crabbe) is tortured by King Vultan in *Flash Gordon*, chapter 6.

quet held by Vultan, Dale proclaims her affection for the King, but as they dine they are interrupted by a mutiny in the furnace room, led by Flash, Barin and Thun.

The revolt is suppressed by the hawkman guards, and Vultan takes Dale and Aura to the furnace room, where Dale screams and faints at the sight of Flash being whipped by the guards. The unconscious girl is taken away by Aura and a hawkman guard, as Vultan orders Flash imprisoned in the "static room."

After Dale regains consciousness, Aura scolds her for her weakness. Vultan arrives and tells Dale he doubts her professed affection for him. Dale tries to reassure him that she no longer cares for Flash, but Vultan, dubious, takes her to the static room. Aura follows. In the static room, Flash has been strapped to a steel brace and suspended between two sparking electrodes. As Vultan forces Dale to watch, high-voltage electricity courses through Flash's body and he slowly loses consciousness...

Comments

The strange ballet sequence representing Vultan's "entertainment" at his banquet is a clip from the 1927 Universal feature *The Midnight Sun*, starring Laura LaPlante. *The Midnight Sun*, like most Universal silents, is a lost film, and the scenes used here represent the only extant footage from the movie.

....

Chapter 7: "Shattering Doom"

Synopsis

As Flash, nearly electrocuted, collapses in Vultan's static room, Dale, still insisting to Vultan that she does not love Flash, faints in horror, and Vultan orders the unconscious girl taken away. Aura appears with a raygun and demands that Vultan release Flash into her custody. Vultan finally understands that Aura wants Flash for herself, and orders his guards to unshackle the Earthman.

As Zarkov experiments with a new anti-gravity ray in Vultan's laboratory, Aura and a hawkman guard arrive with the unconscious Flash, who is revived by Zarkov in an "electrostimulator."

In the throne room, Vultan notices that Dale, who believes that Flash will die because of her, is depressed, and orders one of his guards to have Zarkov report news of Flash's condition. Vultan tries to amuse Dale by casting shadows on the wall and presenting her with opulent jewelry, but she remains dejected, concerned about Flash.

In the laboratory, Zarkov has revived Flash with the electrostimulator. A hawkman guard arrives and orders Zarkov to report to Vultan. After they leave, Aura confronts Flash, demanding his loyalty, and, wielding a blowtorch, threatens to blind him if he refuses. Flash steadfastly insists that he only loves Dale, and Aura, heartbroken, suffers an emotional breakdown. She drops the blowtorch, unable to carry out her threat.

A hawkman guard arrives to take Flash back to the furnace room, but Flash breaks away and returns to Vultan's throne room to rejoin Dale. He struggles with Vultan's guards,

Having rejected Aura, Flash (Buster Crabbe) tries to rescue Dale (Jean Rogers) from Vultan (John Lipson).

but is outnumbered and recaptured, as a laughing Vultan orders him, over Dale's protests, returned to the furnace room.

Zarkov is again summoned from the lab and ordered to bring a coil of electrical wire. The hawkman guards in the furnace room have determined that the rebellious Flash has become a disruptive influence among the slaves and have decided to electrocute him. They order Zarkov to attach a high-voltage wire to Flash's wrist shackle, and Zarkov does this.

Ming has now arrived in the sky city with his rocketship fleet, and Aura tells Vultan that her father has come to demand his obedience. Zarkov stealthily returns to the atom furnace room, disconnecting the electrical wire from Flash's wrist shackle and rewiring it to a shovel. He instructs Flash to hurl the shovel into the atom furnace at the right moment, causing the furnace to explode. In the throne room, Ming criticizes Vultan for defying his authority, but Vultan rebels against Ming, with hawkman guards, brandishing rayguns, entering the throne room.

Again, Flash, Barin and Thun instigate a revolt in the furnace room, and as a struggle breaks out between the hawkmen guards and the slaves, Flash tosses the wired shovel into the furnace just as a hawkman throws the electrical switch, believing that it will kill Flash. Instead, as Flash and his friends race for the safety of a protective lead wall, the atom furnace explodes and Vultan's sky city bursts into flames...

Flash (Buster Crabbe) is imprisoned by Vultan and forced to feed the radium furnaces.

Top: Zarkov attaches an electrical cable to a shovel so that Flash can destroy the furnaces. From left: James Pierce, Buster Crabbe, Frank Shannon, Richard Alexander. *Bottom:* A revolt soon breaks out in the furnace room. From left: James Pierce, Buster Crabbe, Richard Alexander.

The abundantly endowed Princess Aura (Priscilla Lawson) tries to seduce Flash (Buster Crabbe) in chapter 7 of *Flash Gordon*.

Comments

As Ming's rocketship fleet approaches the sky city of the hawkmen, several of Elmer A. Johnson's miniature ships are shown flying in formation, the many wires used to support them hidden by photographing the models in extreme soft focus.

There were more wardrobe problems for Priscilla Lawson during the filming of chapter 7. In the scene in which Aura threatens Flash with a blowtorch, the distraught Aura places her hands atop her head in despair as she drops the torch. The resulting physical strain, combined with the abundant Lawson anatomy, was a bit too much, and Aura's skimpy top bursts open in the back — onscreen — as she exits the frame before (fortunately, or unfortunately, depending on one's point of view) more than the censor would tolerate can be revealed.

. . . .

Chapter 8: "Tournament of Death"

Synopsis

As the enraged Ming confronts Vultan over his defiance, the atom furnace explodes, and, as the power of the gravity-defying rays falter, Vultan's city tilts dangerously in the sky. Flash and Thun burst into the throne room and Flash pulls a sword on Ming, but Dale inadvertently stumbles into Flash and the hawkman guards recapture Flash and Thun, taking them to the execution chamber on Vultan's orders. Flash and Thun are about to be executed by a firing squad when the guards lose their balance as the sky city tilts. Escaping, Flash and Thun run back to the throne room.

Zarkov arrives and reveals that he has discovered a new anti-gravity ray that can save Vultan's city, but that he will use it only if he and his friends are granted their freedom. Vultan agrees, and Zarkov leads them all to the laboratory where he activates the ray, restoring the sky city to its former elevation in the clouds. Vultan, honoring his word, frees them, but Ming objects and calls a "Tournament of Death," decreeing that Flash will have to fight for his life against "the Mighty Masked Swordsman of Mongo."

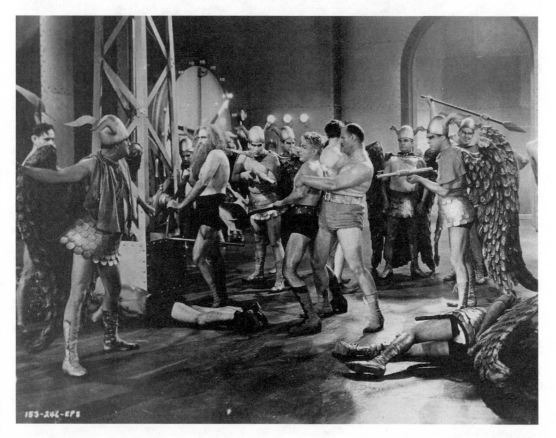

Pandemonium in the furnace room! James Pierce, Buster Crabbe and Richard Alexander are in the center.

Top: With the anti-gravity support beams faltering, the sky city begins to tip dangerously. From left: James Pierce, Priscilla Lawson, Jean Rogers, Buster Crabbe, John Lipson, Charles Middleton, Earl Askam. *Bottom:* As panic grips Vultan's throne room, Zarkov announces the discovery of a new ray that can save the city. From left: John Lipson, Buster Crabbe, Jean Rogers.

Top: Flash (Buster Crabbe, center) is forced to enter the Tournament of Death. *Botom:* Flash (Buster Crabbe) learns that Barin (Richard Alexander) secretly loves Princess Aura.

Flash (Buster Crabbe) is forced to fight the savage Orangopoid (Ray Corrigan).

In the arena, Flash battles the masked swordsman, and after a tense duel unmasks his opponent as none other than Prince Barin, who explains that he was forced into fighting Flash. Later, in private, Barin admits to Flash that he had hoped to wound Flash sufficiently to satisfy Ming—or that Flash would kill him and put an end to his misery, confessing that he is in love with Princess Aura.

Ming now demands that Flash battle "the Mighty Beast of Mongo" in the arena. Thun objects but is overruled, and Vultan, now in total sympathy with Flash and his friends, reminds Ming that if the Earthman wins, he is entitled to his freedom and the bride of his choice.

Flash once again enters the arena, only to be confronted by a huge and powerful gorilla-like horned beast, an "orangopoid." Flash grapples with the savage animal but is overcome by the beast's superior strength. Bloodied and exhausted, Flash sinks to the floor of the arena as the orangopoid bears down on him, tearing at his throat...

Comments

Veteran serial director Ray Taylor worked on this episode, without billing. The savage orangopoid was played by Ray "Crash" Corrigan (1902–1976), a "B"-Western cowboy star (most notably in the *Three Mesquiteers* and the *Range Busters* series) who had a profitable sideline portraying gorillas in movies. Corrigan's gorilla suit was modified here with the addition of a unicorn-style horn attached to the head. Because he was under contract to Republic Pictures at the time, Corrigan performed in *Flash Gordon* anonymously, without screen credit.

He also played the heroic lead in a rival production, Republic's 12-chapter serial *Undersea Kingdom* (1936), which was a blatant imitation of *Flash Gordon*. A watchable but inferior serial, *Undersea Kingdom* went into release about a month after *Flash Gordon*. Late in his career, Corrigan also played the title role in the minor sci-fi classic *It! The Terror from Beyond Space* (United Artists, 1958).

Remembering the *Flash Gordon* orangopoid scene with Corrigan, Buster Crabbe recalled that Corrigan had requested that a group of young girls should be present on the set to reach inside his ape suit and wipe him off at regular intervals, since he perspired heavily inside the costume. Crabbe observed that Corrigan seemed to undergo this routine with increasing frequency, obviously enjoying the procedure! [*Interview*].

....

Chapter 9: "Fighting the Fire Dragon"

Synopsis

As Flash battles for his life against the orangopoid, Aura asks Ming's high priest if there is any way the orangopoid can be slain in combat, and he tells her the legend of a vulnerable white spot on the beast's throat. Grabbing a spear from one of the guards, Aura enters the arena and gives Flash the spear. He kills the orangopoid, and Ming, though enraged, is bound by the rules of the tournament to grant each warrior, Flash and Barin, their freedom and the right to wed the bride of their choice in a festival to be held in his

Top: Flash (Buster Crabbe) is nearly killed by the Orangopoid (Ray Corrigan). *Bottom:* Princess Aura helps Flash to defeat the Orangopoid. Buster Crabbe (left) and Priscilla Lawson.

palace. Seething with anger, Ming leaves the throne room and Vultan's sky city, returning to his own domain. Thun, refusing to enter Ming's palace for the festival, also leaves Vultan's city, returning to his own kingdom.

Back in Ming's palace, Ming continues to secretly plot against the Earth people with his high priest, ordering him to eliminate Flash one way or another; while in the palace laboratory, Zarkov tries, unsuccessfully, to contact Earth. As Flash and Dale share a private romantic moment, kissing on the eve of the festival, they are secretly watched by Aura, heartbroken as she sees their genuine love for each other. But Aura herself is being spied upon, by Ming's high priest, who surprises the princess as she watches Flash and Dale, and who then conspires with her to give Flash "drops of forgetfulness"—pills that will rob him of his memory. Realizing that Flash will then forget Dale, Aura agrees, planning to take Flash through the Tunnel of Terror to the palace of the Great God Tao, where she will have him to herself at last.

As Zarkov continues his attempts to contact Earth, one of Ming's soldiers, secretly acting under Aura's orders, delivers goblets of drugged wine to Flash and Barin in their quarters, telling them that it is a present from King Vultan. Flash and Barin drink the wine, falling unconscious, and Aura, with the high priest and a group of Ming's soldiers, arrive and carry Flash away on a stretcher. Zarkov sneaks away from the laboratory to tell Flash that he is receiving signals from Earth, but finds Flash gone and Barin unconscious.

Flash's friends learn that he has been drugged. From left: Frank Shannon, Jean Rogers, Richard Alexander, John Lipson.

Barin awakens and tells Zarkov that he doesn't know what happened — that he and Flash had been drinking wine sent by King Vultan. Vultan arrives and tells them that he had not sent wine. They discover a scarf that is determined to be Princess Aura's, and Barin and Vultan find the soldier who had delivered the wine, forcing him to tell the truth about Aura's plans. Barin, Zarkov, Dale and Vultan then set out in pursuit of Aura, whose party is taking the unconscious Flash through the Tunnel of Terror to the palace of The Great God Tao.

They follow Aura, the high priest and the soldiers into the Tunnel of Terror, and even though the high priest assures Aura that the fire monster, guardian of the tunnel, is asleep and will not attack them, he double-crosses the princess and sounds a gong, awakening the beast. As the fire monster, spewing flame and smoke, approaches the unconscious Flash, Aura screams in helpless terror, just as Barin, Zarkov, Dale and Vultan arrive to see what is happening...

Comments

For this episode, the giant lobster-clawed cave monster (or "Gocko"), last seen (and defeated) in chapter 3, was re-designed somewhat, with flame-producing tubing, to represent the Fire Monster.

Priscilla Lawson's acting in the scene showing Aura secretly watching Flash and Dale as they kiss is excellent, with both actress and script displaying an emotional texture rare in serials. Her character, as well as John Lipson's King Vultan, changes emotionally and undergoes a moral shift across the serial's story arc; this sort of characterization is only one of many factors that make *Flash Gordon* a very atypical (and far superior) serial.

·····················

Chapter 10: "The Unseen Peril"

Synopsis

As the fire monster attacks, bearing down on the unconscious Flash, Zarkov produces a hand grenade and throws it, killing the monster. Zarkov, Barin, Dale and Vultan take Flash back to the palace, where Flash revives, suffering from amnesia. Flash is compelled to choose his bride at the arranged ceremony, but, unable to remember, goes away with Aura. Vultan protests but is imprisoned by Ming. Dale, shocked and heartbroken by this turn of events, is comforted by Barin as Ming makes his carnal intentions toward her clear.

Below the palace, Vultan is thrown into a dungeon cell. In the laboratory, Barin reports what has transpired to Zarkov, and Zarkov tells Barin to get Flash to the laboratory so that his memory can be restored as quickly as possible. Meanwhile, Flash, who is with Dale and Aura, cannot remember Dale at all, and believes Aura when she deceitfully tells him that he loves her. Grief-stricken, Dale leaves the room, but Barin arrives, and when Aura lies and tells Flash that Barin has come to harm her, Flash draws his sword and challenges Barin to a duel. Zarkov appears and restrains Flash while Barin knocks him unconscious. As Aura flees, they take Flash back to the laboratory, and Zarkov restores his memory with a ray machine.

Top: His memory erased by the drug, Flash believes that Prince Barin is his enemy. From left: Buster Crabbe, Priscilla Lawson, Richard Alexander, Jean Rogers. *Bottom:* Flash is knocked unconscious by Prince Barin. From left: Richard Alexander, Buster Crabbe, Frank Shannon, Jean Rogers.

Top: Flash's memory is restored by Zarkov. From left: Jean Rogers, Buster Crabbe, Frank Shannon. *Bottom:* Zarkov (Frank Shannon) receives a message from Earth as Dale (Jean Rogers) looks on.

Ming's soldiers prepare to execute Flash. From center left: Earl Askam, Buster Crabbe, Frank Shannon, Jean Rogers, Richard Alexander.

As Flash begins to revive, Professor Gordon, at Dorr Observatory on Earth, tries to communicate with Mongo and finally connects with Zarkov in the laboratory, but the radio signal fades and is lost.

Meanwhile, Aura confers with Ming, telling him that the Earth people are in the laboratory. Ming dispatches his soldiers to kill Flash, over Aura's protests.

Flash, his memory fully restored, has now revived, and Officer Torch, leading Ming's soldiers, bursts into the lab and orders Flash to stand against the wall so that he can be executed immediately — or his friends will die with him. Flash obeys, and as Zarkov presses a switch on a nearby control panel Flash suddenly vanishes...

Comments

This episode begins a subplot in which Flash is rendered invisible by Zarkov, a sequence that was adapted from Raymond's original comic strip. Invisibility was a frequent plot device in horror and fantasy movies of the 1930s and 40s (it was easy to achieve, since it involved showing nothing), and had figured most prominently in director James Whale's 1933 classic *The Invisible Man*, also made and released by Universal. Other serials using the concept included *The Vanishing Shadow* (Universal, 1934), *The Phantom Creeps* (Universal, 1939) and *The Invisible Monster* (Republic, 1950).

······················

Chapter 11: "In the Claws of the Tigron"

Synopsis

As Flash vanishes from sight, Ming's soldiers, sent to execute him, flee in terror. Flash has been turned invisible by a ray machine Zarkov has invented in Ming's own laboratory. To demonstrate, Zarkov momentarily restores Flash to visibility, then, at Flash's insistence, makes him invisible again.

Flash, unseen, secretly enters Ming's throne room, where Officer Torch and Ming's soldiers are reporting this turn of events to a skeptical Ming. The invisible Flash begins strangling Ming on his own throne, and then fights and overpowers Ming's soldiers. Leaving the throne room, Flash warns Ming to leave him and his friends alone or suffer the consequences.

Ming, stunned, refuses to listen when his high priest tries to blame Flash's invisibility on "the vengeance of the Great God Tao," and promptly orders the deranged cleric imprisoned. Ming orders Officer Torch to destroy the invisibility machine, and Torch leaves with his soldiers to obey.

Flash experiences the effects of Zarkov's invisibility machine. From left: Buster Crabbe, Frank Shannon, Jean Rogers, Richard Alexander.

Dale expresses her concern for Flash. From left: Frank Shannon, Jean Rogers, Richard Alexander.

Meanwhile, as a guard delivers food to King Vultan in his dungeon prison, the invisible Flash arrives and, overpowering the guard, frees Vultan, who follows him back to the laboratory. In the throne room, as Ming cowers in fear, his soldiers arrive and tell him of Vultan's escape.

In the laboratory, Zarkov restores Flash to visibility as Barin, Dale and Vultan watch. Zarkov tells them that he plans to take power magazines to the rocketship so that they can escape Ming, fly to Vultan's sky city, and from there return to Earth. Zarkov then finally makes radio contact with Professor Gordon on Earth. Zarkov makes Flash invisible again, as Aura, from a secret post within the laboratory walls, listens using a concealed microphone. Barin stays in the laboratory with Dale to protect her while the invisible Flash, along with Barin, Zarkov and Vultan, carry the power magazines to the rocketship.

Aura sends a guard to tell Ming that Dale and Barin are in the laboratory, but Barin has noticed the microphone Aura has been using to eavesdrop. He takes Dale away to the caves below the palace for protection. Aura reports to Ming in the throne room, and tells him that Barin has taken Dale to the subterranean caves.

As Barin leaves Dale in the caves and hurries away to inform Flash and the others, Aura and the Mistress of the Sacred Tigron use the feline beast to search for the Earth girl in the catacombs.

Zarkov, the invisible Flash and Vultan return to the laboratory, only to see that Barin and Dale are gone. They are attacked by Ming's soldiers, who arrive at the lab under Ming's orders. As they struggle, Flash regains his visibility just as Barin arrives and tells him where he has hidden Dale.

In the caves below, the Tigron, sensing Dale's presence, breaks away from Aura and the Tigron Mistress, and, locating Dale, ferociously pounces on her as she screams in terror...

Comments

The sequence showing Aura and the Tigron Mistress (Sana Raya) leading the beast (a regular tiger) through the subterranean caves is compromised somewhat by the obvious use of stunt doubles substituting for the actresses. A double was also used for Jean Rogers when the Tigron attacked her. Some footage of the tiger was from Universal's stock library, and had been seen previously in serials like *Tarzan, the Tiger* (1929).

....

Chapter 12: "Trapped in the Turret"

Synopsis

As the Tigron attacks Dale, Flash arrives with Barin and kills the beast, strangling it with his bare hands. Unseen, Ming is watching on a spaceograph. As the distraught Tigron Mistress flees, Barin confronts Aura, expressing his love for her, and convinces her to help the Earth people instead of trying to win Flash by murdering the girl he loves. Undergoing a sudden but sincere change of heart, Aura agrees.

In the laboratory, the fight between Zarkov, Vultan and Ming's soldiers continues, with the soldiers finally gaining the upper hand; but Zarkov refuses to divulge the secret of his invisibility machine to Ming. Flash and Dale warily accept Aura's offer of friendship, and Aura promises to intercede with her father on their behalf. They go to Ming's throne room, and Barin, drawing his sword, threatens Ming, but offers to live in peace with him as he announces his love for Aura. Back in the laboratory, Ming's soldiers destroy Zarkov's invisibility machine, over the scientist's protests.

Ming, delighted to learn of Barin's affection for Aura, agrees to let the Earth people leave Mongo, and also proclaims Zarkov and Vultan free, announcing that they will proceed with the aborted wedding feast. Flash, Dale, Barin and Aura return to the laboratory to give Zarkov and Vultan the news of their freedom, only to find that the invisibility machine has been destroyed. Zarkov then communicates with Professor Gordon on Earth, and is able to report that they are safe and planning a return flight before the radio signal is once again disrupted.

King Vultan, suspicious of Ming's true intentions, suggests that they all return to his sky city, from which Flash, Dale and Zarkov can return to Earth. The others agree. As Ming's soldiers, acting on his orders, spy on the Earth people, Barin prepares his rocketship to carry his friends to Vultan's city. Ming's soldiers report this to the emperor, and as Barin takes off in his rocketship to meet the Earth people at a predetermined location

Zarkov radios Earth. From left: John Lipson, Buster Crabbe, Jean Rogers, Frank Shannon, Richard Alexander.

at the Lake of Rocks, Flash and his friends communicate with Thun on the spaceograph and tell him to meet them in Vultan's sky city.

Flash, Dale, Vultan and Aura rendezvous at a cave near the Lake of Rocks, awaiting Barin's arrival, but when the rocketship appears, they are shocked when it suddenly angles downward toward them, firing explosive rays directly at them...

Comments

Apparently, chapter 12 came up a little short in the final editing, and is padded out with seemingly endless shots of Ming's soldiers marching through the caverns (taken from chapter 2), machine lights flashing, and rocketships taking off— to the extent that the narrative flow almost becomes confusing, with the "giant" lizards from the first chapter even inserted at one point, ostensibly looking upward and roaring at a rocketship as it flies overhead!

Flash and his friends await the arrival of Prince Barin's rocketship. From left: Frank Shannon, Priscilla Lawson, John Lipson, Jean Rogers, Buster Crabbe.

....

Chapter 13: "Rocketing to Earth"

Synopsis

Shocked and confused by the attack from Barin's ship, Flash and his friends take shelter inside a nearby cave, escaping through a trap door known to Aura just as the cave explodes. Ming, who has Barin in chains, watches this on a spaceograph and orders Barin taken away. Flash and his friends survive the explosion, but Vultan is injured. As they stealthily make their way through the cavern, they see Prince Barin — a chained prisoner — being led away by Ming's soldiers, and realize that he was never in the rocketship.

Flash attacks the soldiers, freeing Barin, and they all return to the laboratory. One of the soldiers reports this to Ming, and in the laboratory Flash frees Barin from his chains as Zarkov attends to Vultan's wounds. Officer Torch, acting on Ming's orders, tries to enter the laboratory with a contingent of soldiers, but finds that the laboratory door has been charged with thousands of volts of electricity by Zarkov. Ming arrives and tells his men to cut off the main power generator supplying electricity to the laboratory, and they do

Top: Flash and his friends are taken into custody by Ming's guards. From left: Glenn Strange, Buster Crabbe, Jean Rogers, Frank Shannon, Richard Alexander, Priscilla Lawson. *Bottom:* The High Priest announces Ming's death. From left: Buster Crabbe, Theodore Lorch, Priscilla Lawson, Richard Alexander, James Pierce.

this. But suddenly a siren warns of an air attack against the palace, forcing Ming to return to his throne room, where he learns he is under attack by Thun's gyroships.

Ming's soldiers destroy the laboratory door with a raygun, seizing the Earth people, Aura, and Vultan, and taking them to Ming's throne room. Watching the air battle on the spaceograph, Ming sees that his forces are losing—just as Thun and his savage lion men burst into the throne room. Ming flees his own throne room, running into the caverns, as Flash, Barin and Thun, followed by Aura, pursue him. Reaching the palace of the Great God Tao, Ming conspires with his high priest to commit suicide, and enters through the portals, with smoke apparently consuming him.

Flash, Thun, Barin and Aura arrive, and learn of Ming's demise from the high priest. They return to the palace with a heartbroken Aura. In Ming's laboratory, Zarkov converses with Professor Gordon on Earth, as the high priest secretly watches from the shadows, and announces that he, Flash and Dale will soon be returning home. As the Earth people leave the laboratory, the high priest, now completely deranged, prepares a small but lethal bomb.

As the Earth people are honored in the throne room by Aura, now established as ruler

Flash, Dale and Zarkov prepare for their voyage home. From left: John Lipson, Frank Shannon, Jean Rogers, Buster Crabbe, Priscilla Lawson, James Pierce.

Flash disposes of a bomb planted by Ming's High Priest. From left: Frank Shannon, Buster Crabbe, Jean Rogers.

of Mongo, she prevails upon them not to attempt the dangerous return flight to Earth, but to remain on Mongo. Zarkov, however, insists that they must return to Earth, "for the benefit of science." The high priest, cackling maniacally, plants the bomb aboard Zarkov's rocketship, hiding nearby just as the Earth people arrive with Aura, Barin and Vultan to begin their return space voyage. They exchange farewells with their friends and board the rocketship, blasting off just as the high priest steps out of hiding and smugly declares what he has done to Aura, Barin and Vultan. As Vultan strangles the madman in a rage, Aura and Barin hurry back to a radio in an attempt to warn the Earth people.

Back in the palace laboratory, Aura, Barin and Vultan are able, after some difficulty, to establish radio contact with Zarkov's rocketship and warn the Earth people about the bomb. Flash and Zarkov search for and discover it, hurling it through the rocketship door into outer space just before it explodes.

They radio their friends on Mongo that they are safe and on their way home. On Earth, Zarkov's rocketship is sighted as it approaches, causing world-wide excitement, and as the craft prepares to land, Flash and Dale share a passionate kiss, having triumphantly survived their perilous adventures on Mongo.

Flash (Buster Crabbe) and Dale (Jean Rogers) in Ming's laboratory.

Comments

And so the greatest movie serial ever made concludes, not with a weak and unsatisfying ending as most of them do, but with a strong and memorable emotional highpoint.

The last episode is the first episode in which we see any lion men other than Thun. Judging by their behavior in the final battle with Ming's soldiers (with one of them clearly going for a man's throat), they are an especially bloodthirsty race.

Director Stephani neglected to shoot enough coverage for the scene in Ming's laboratory just before Flash and friends are taken to the throne room, filming the action from only one angle, a medium-long shot. Probably a result of the rushed schedule, this oversight necessitated the frame having to be optically cropped and enlarged in the lab to provide an alternate shot for editing. The optically cropped "blow-up" shots in this scene are recognizable by their darker contrast.

Two:
Flash Gordon's Trip to Mars (1938)

PRODUCTION CREDITS

Flash Gordon's Trip to Mars (Universal) Released March 21, 1938. *Associate Producer*: Barney A. Sarecky, *Directors*: Ford Beebe, Robert F. Hill, *Screenplay*: Herbert Dalmas, Wyndham Gittens, Norman S. Hall, Ray Trampe, *Photography*: Jerry Ash, A.S.C., *Art Director*: Ralph M. DeLacey, *Film Editors*: Joseph Gluck, Saul A. Goodkind, Louis Sackin, Alvin Todd, *Dialogue Director*: Sarah C. Haney. *Assistant Directors*: George Webster, Eddie Tyler, Les Warner, *Assistant Cameramen*: William Sickner, Lloyd Wright, Michael Walsh, *Miniatures*: Glen Johnson, *Makeup*: Jim Collins, *Props*: Eddie Keyes, Charles Fowler, *Sound*: William Hedgecock, John Kemp, *Men's Wardrobe*: Shirley Ware, *Ladies' Wardrobe*: M. Berneman, *Still Photography*: Eddie Jones, Sherman Clark, *Unit Manager*: George Webster, *Sound System*: Western Electric. Running Time: 301 minutes (Note: The DVD available from Image Entertainment is slightly abridged, missing 90 seconds of footage in Chapter 3. The running time listed here is for the complete serial.)

CHAPTER TITLES

(1) "New Worlds to Conquer," (2) "The Living Dead," (3) "Queen of Magic," (4) "Ancient Enemies," (5) "The Boomerang," (6) "Tree-Men of Mars," (7) "The Prisoner of Mongo," (8) "The Black Sapphire of Kalu," (9) "Symbol of Death," (10) "Incense of Forgetfulness," (11) "Human Bait," (12) "Ming the Merciless," (13) "The Miracle of Magic," (14) "A Beast at Bay," (15) "An Eye for an Eye"

CAST

Larry "Buster" Crabbe (*Flash Gordon*), Jean Rogers (*Dale Arden*), Charles Middleton (*Ming, the Merciless*), Frank Shannon (*Dr. Alexis Zarkov*), Donald Kerr ("*Happy*" *Hapgood*), Beatrice Roberts (*Queen Azura*), Richard Alexander (*Prince Barin*), C. Montague Shaw (*Clay King*), Wheeler Oakman (*Tarnak*), Kenneth Duncan (*airdrome commander*), Warner P. Richmond (*Zandar*), Jack Mulhall (*stratosled pilot*), Anthony Warde (*Mighty Toran, king of the forest people*), Lane Chandler (*death squadron commander*), Ben Lewis (*Martian pilot*), Hooper Atchley (*Dr. DuNord*), James G. Blaine (*Professor Richter*), Thomas Carr (*Capt. Rama of the forest people*), Wheaton Chambers (*bit part*), George De Normand (*bit part*), Earl Douglas (*bit part*), James C. Eagles (*bit part*), Jerry Frank (*soldier*), Jerry Gardner (*bit part*), Herbert Holcombe (*bit part*), Reed Howes (*bit part*), Fred Kohler, Jr. (*soldier*), Louis Merrill (*bit part*), Eddie Parker (*bit part*), Stanley Price (*soldier turned to clay*), Kane Richmond (*stratosled captain*), Edwin Stanley (*General Rankin*), Tom Steele (*bit part*),

Al Bridge (*Martian*), Ray Turner (*Zarkov's servant*), Bud Wolfe (*bit part*), Eddie Parker (*bit part*), Loren Riebe (*bit part*), Sid Dawson (*bit part*).

FEATURE VERSIONS

Mars Attacks the World (released theatrically November 2, 1938, running time 68 minutes) and *The Deadly Ray from Mars* (1966, running time 99 minutes), distributed for television syndication and non-theatrical rentals.

VIDEO AVAILABILITY

Both the complete serial, *Flash Gordon's Trip to Mars*, and the feature version *The Deadly Ray from Mars* have been released on DVD by Image Entertainment. *Mars Attacks the World* has been released on DVD by Sinister Cinema.

....

Chapter 1: "New Worlds to Conquer"

Synopsis

A powerful radio signal is received by Williams Observatory from the Zarkov expedition, returning from the planet Mongo after saving the Earth from Ming the Merciless. After the rocketship is positively identified, heading toward earth at 1,200 miles per hour, the news is released to the world.

Doctor Zarkov, Flash Gordon and Dale Arden brace for a rough landing as their rocketship enters the atmosphere, and the craft finally comes to rest near a farmhouse in the midwestern United States. The three heroes are welcomed back with a tickertape parade and front page headlines. Giving a speech before a fascinated audience, Dr. Zarkov recounts their adventures on Mongo, and comments that, judging from the advanced science he observed on Mongo, the world must be prepared for the possibility of an invasion from outer space.

On the planet Mars, a sinister light beam is emitted from a huge, powerful lamp and knifes across the void of space toward Earth. Two alien beings materialize on Earth as the light beam strikes, and plant a strange mechanical device in the ground just as they perish in agony and vanish from sight. As Ming the Merciless (still alive) and Azura, Queen of Mars, watch these events on Mars through a telescopic viewer and coldly discuss their plans for the destruction of Earth, the device planted by the Martians emits a strange vapor that seeps into Earth's atmosphere. Violent storms and earthquakes suddenly occur, threatening civilization, and a panel of scientific experts, meeting to discuss the catastrophe, fails to reach agreement on the cause of the destruction.

Happy Hapgood, an ambitious newspaper reporter attending the conference, ascertains that Dr. Zarkov would probably be able to determine the cause of the disasters. Hapgood tricks Zarkov's servant into supplying the phone number where Zarkov, in seclusion with Flash Gordon and Dale Arden while conducting research, can be reached.

At Zarkov's research facility in the countryside, Dale Arden watches anxiously through binoculars as Flash and Zarkov fly a plane at 20,000 feet in an effort to photograph, with an infrared camera, the beam of light striking the Earth. Their plane is suddenly affected by the light beam and spins out of control. Flash and Zarkov bail out, taking the exposed film with them, and land safely in the countryside as Dale rushes out to meet them and Happy Hapgood emerges from hiding, taking their picture. Happy tries to follow them back to Zarkov's lab to get an interview, but is entangled in a barbed-wire fence by Flash and left behind.

Zarkov, developing the exposed film, determines that the beam of light striking Earth is causing the violent atmospheric disruptions threatening mankind, and believes that the ray is emanating from Mongo. He resolves to travel there in his rocketship to save civilization, and Flash and Dale agree to go with him. Together they blast off for Mongo in Zarkov's rocketship, only to discover, once they have left Earth, that Happy Hapgood has stowed away onboard.

On Mars, Queen Azura is at war with the Clay People, a strange, gnome-like race living in nearby caves who were transformed from normal men into clay men through her sinister magic. Officiating at the trial of a saboteur who has attempted to prevent her war with the Clay People, Azura transforms him into a clay man, and with a gesture of her hand he vanishes from sight. Azura disappears by magic and reappears before Ming in her laboratory. Just then a huge pipe malfunctions, erupting in flames; Ming walks through the fire, throwing a switch that dampens the flames and saves them. Together, Ming and Azura discuss their plans for conquest.

Happy Hapgood, a newspaper reporter, stows away aboard Zarkov's rocketship. From left: Donald Kerr, Buster Crabbe, Frank Shannon, Jean Rogers.

Zarkov's rocketship is struck by the Martian ray. From left: Donald Kerr, Jean Rogers, Frank Shannon, Buster Crabbe.

As Zarkov's rocketship approaches Mongo, the spacecraft is suddenly diverted away from Mongo and speeds toward Mars. Zarkov finally realizes, from closer observation, that the ray is being projected from Mars, not Mongo, and as the rocketship strikes the powerful beam it malfunctions, hurtling out of control toward the Martian surface far below...

Comments

Keeping in mind the excessive cost of *Flash Gordon*, Universal's serial unit made herculean efforts to minimize expenses on *Flash Gordon's Trip to Mars*. A studio memo dated October 13, 1937, from Universal executive E. A. Tambert to studio manager Martin F. Murray and executive Val Paul states that Tambert had gone over the *Trip to Mars* script with associate producer Barney Sarecky and felt that costs could be held down to $150,000. This soon proved to be a naively optimistic estimate, with the story's fantastic subject matter and epic sweep demanding a greater financial commitment. The budget was finally approved at $168,700. Even this figure proved inadequate, though, and *Flash Gordon's Trip to Mars* was completed, after five weeks of principal photography, at a final cost of $182,000.

The serial's budget provided for the following allocations:

Cast	$15,200
Screenplay	$5,350
Set Construction	$19,750
Special Effects	$6,950
Wardrobe	$2,800
Music and Sound Effects	$1,000

The lead actors' weekly salaries were stipulated as follows:

Buster Crabbe	$400 per week
Jean Rogers	$250 per week
Charles Middleton	$500 per week
Donald Kerr	$200 per week
Richard Alexander	$175 per week
Beatrice Roberts	Flat Fee

Although Charles Middleton earned the highest weekly salary at $500 per week, he was only contracted for two weeks, whereas Buster Crabbe had been signed for 8 weeks, earning a total of $3,200. This made Crabbe the highest-paid cast member (Crabbe filmed the Universal serial *Red Barry* concurrently with *Mars*). Beatrice Roberts was not paid a weekly salary, receiving only a flat fee for her services. *Flash Gordon's Trip to Mars* began

Charles Middleton and Buster Crabbe in a publicity photo for *Flash Gordon's Trip to Mars* (1938).

shooting on November 15, 1937, with a few days of miniature work using a skeleton crew before principal photography with the actors started on November 19 at 7:30 A.M. The actors finished their last scenes on the afternoon of December 24, 1937.

The miniature work, unfinished at this point, picked up again, and was essentially completed by December 30, although some minor effects work and trick optical printing was not finished until early in the first week of January 1938.

Flash Gordon's Trip to Mars was in production for a total of 31 working days involving principal photography, a real testament to the compartmentalized studio efficiency of the day, especially considering the serial's physical attributes and total running time of just over 5 hours!

Flash Gordon's Trip to Mars was partially based on a Big Little Book entitled *Flash Gordon and the Witch Queen of Mongo*, printed by Whitman Publishing Co. of Racine, Wisconsin, in 1936. This was Big Little Book number 1190 and was 424 pages long. Divided into 12 chapters, it featured 198 panels of Alex Raymond artwork illustrating the story. Little seems to have been used from the Big Little Book plot besides the Queen Azura character, who does not die in the book as she does in the serial. The book, for instance (as its title indicates), takes place on Mongo, not Mars. Exactly why the location for the story was changed by the filmmakers from Mongo to Mars is unclear. The serial was originally mentioned in the trade press under the Big Little Book title *Flash Gordon and the Witch Queen of Mongo*. Some commentators have asserted that the notoriety of Orson Welles' *War of the Worlds* radio broadcast was responsible, but since the infamous Welles broadcast was made on October 30, 1938, and *Flash Gordon's Trip to Mars* was filmed in late 1937 and released in March of 1938, this is clearly impossible. The Welles program did influence the title and release date of the *feature* version, *Mars Attacks the World* (released on November 2, 1938). Ironically, in all likelihood, the wide popularity *of Flash Gordon's Trip to Mars* earlier in the year may have influenced Orson Welles in his choice of broadcast material! As mentioned in the introduction, the feature version, *Mars Attacks the World*, had originally been made under the title *Rocket Ship*. An April 1938 release date was scheduled. It was then shelved by Universal and hurriedly retitled *Mars Attacks the World* after Welles' broadcast, with the title *Rocket Ship* transferred to the feature version of the first serial. This caused a mix-up in photo material used in ads and posters, with images from one serial feature used to advertise the other, resulting in a lot of confusion over the years. Even the American Film Institute catalog, drawing their information from Universal files that were apparently never amended to reflect the title changes, is foggy on this issue.

Made at the same time as the serial, *Mars Attacks the World* contains several shots not used in the serial, including opening stock footage of an observatory telescope studying the heavens and a few miniature shots that were filmed in an apparent attempt to upgrade the serial's often patchy special effects. These include a more detailed view of Queen Azura's Martian city, a more convincing representation of the nitron beam striking the Earth, and an impressive view of Zarkov's rocketship taking off from Earth, with a city rear-projected behind the miniature.

One of the Martian stratosled miniatures was the only *Flash Gordon* rocketship models known to have survived the original productions; for some time it was on display in the offices of Hollywood's Howard A. Anderson Optical Co.—until it was damaged and inadvertently thrown away by a company employee.

In chapter 1 of *Flash Gordon's Trip to Mars* Dr. Zarkov (Frank Shannon), Dale Arden (Jean Rogers) and Flash Gordon (Buster Crabbe) return to Earth from their previous adventure.

The serial itself was originally released with at least *some* of the prints struck on Kodak Sonochrome Verdante film stock, which produced a green tint. Universal executives must have liked the effect; later the same year they reissued *Dracula* and *Frankenstein*, with a few prints struck on the same green-toned stock. While some filmgoers, such as the late film historian George Turner, have vivid recollections of seeing *Flash Gordon's Trip to Mars* (as well as *Dracula* and *Frankenstein*) in this tinted form in 1938, others have recalled seeing all three films the same year in black-and-white; obviously, not *all* of the release prints for these films were made on color stock. The green-toned prints were probably reserved for more prestigious, big-city engagements and have not been seen since 1938.

The disaster scenes in the serial were stock footage pulled from newsreels and features like *The Shock* (1923) and *Looking for Trouble* (1935).

While in some instances a noticeable effort was made to preserve continuity with the first serial (although difficult to see beneath their capes, Flash, Dale and Zarkov sport the same costumes that they wore in the last chapter of the first serial when they return to Earth in chapter 1 of *Mars*), this attention to detail was, oddly, ignored in other ways (in the same scene, the interior of the rocketship has been completely re-designed, and Jean Rogers — in compliance with the comic strip — has changed from a blonde to a brunette). Other continuity errors include Zarkov and friends returning to Earth in one of Ming's rocketships from the first serial instead of Zarkov's rocketship (the *Just Imagine* miniature), and Zarkov's first name changing from Hans to Alexis (as in the comic strip).

Jerry Ash, A.S.C., the primary cinematographer for *Mars*, photographed several of the Martian scenes through an infra-red filter, producing a startling contrast shift that made the shots more "otherworldly." Ash's photography of the miniatures was a bit more rushed than in the first serial, resulting in plenty of wobbly rocketship movements, but most of his work is equal to that in the original film. Particularly striking is his shot of the Clay People slowly emerging from a cavern wall. This was accomplished by executing a slow dissolve in the camera; since the costumes worn by the actors are the same shade of gray as the cave wall, they appear to "emerge" from their rocky surroundings. The same footage was simply printed in reverse to achieve the opposite effect and show the Clay People fading *into* the wall. Scored with bizarre music lifted from Franz Waxman's score for *Bride of Frankenstein* (Waxman's excellent *Bride* score is used throughout *Mars*), the effect is unforgettable. The "light bridge," a pulsating, horizontal beam of light that the actors appear to walk across, was created by having the actors walk across a wooden plank, then optically printing the animated beam of light over the image.

Many of the physical effects were created by Eddie Keyes, who invented a method for destroying, on camera, first a Martian idol and then a sculpture in Ming's laboratory. This involved pouring iron filings into a mold and then magnetizing them with an electromagnet located below the object, out of camera range. The mold was then removed, with the iron filings retaining the desired shape. When the electricity powering the electromagnet was cut off, the object lost its shape and — whether supposedly struck by a disintegrator beam or death ray — "crumbled" to dust on camera.

Art director Ralph DeLacey created sets for Mars that are quite different from those seen in the first serial, with garishly-shaded palace walls and futuristic metal doors that open in a bizarre "S" pattern. Also impressive are some full-scale Martian stratosleds and rocketships, and the expansive forest kingdom set, photographed outdoors and backed by a painted cyclorama.

An elaborate glass painting augments Queen Azura's Martian throne room, while certain components of the first serial, such as the large backdrop painting of Ming's mountaintop city and clips of a rocketship in flight, are reused in *Trip to Mars*. The miniatures of Thun's gyroships from the first serial turn up again here — used to add detail to instrument panels in the Martian stratosleds! For a series of films with an interplanetary backdrop, it's amazing to note that *Flash Gordon's Trip to Mars* contains the only scenes, in all three serials, of a rocketship flying in outer space against an actual starfield. Even at that, the shot looks cheaply done, as it was achieved by simply double-printing the ship miniature over the stars (resulting in a transparent "ghosting" effect), and is used only in chapters 1 and 15.

The film also seems to have been influenced by the science-fiction pulp magazines of the era — several aliens, used only as peripheral characters, have large, oversized heads (rubber masks) similar to aliens seen in much later science fiction movies.

Flash Gordon's Trip to Mars was co-directed by Ford Beebe (1888–1978) and Robert F. Hill (1886–1966), both veteran serial hands who had been with Universal since the silent era. Besides *Flash Gordon's Trip to Mars* and the sequel, *Flash Gordon Conquers the Universe*, the prolific Beebe's serial credits include *The Shadow of the Eagle* (Mascot, 1932) and

Buster Crabbe, as Flash, on one of art director Ralph DeLacey's Martian sets for *Flash Gordon's Trip to Mars* (1938).

The Adventures of Rex and Rinty (Mascot, 1935). Beebe also directed or co-directed the following for Universal: *Ace Drummond* (1936), *Jungle Jim* (1937), *Radio Patrol* (1937), *Secret Agent X-9* (1937), *Tim Tyler's Luck* (1937), *Wild West Days* (1937), *Red Barry* (1938), *Buck Rogers* (1939), *The Oregon Trail* (1939), *The Phantom Creeps* (1939), *The Green Hornet* (1940), *The Green Hornet Strikes Again* (1940), *Junior G-Men* (1940), *Don Winslow of the Navy* (1941), *Riders of Death Valley* (1941), *Sea Raiders* (1941), *Sky Raiders* (1941), *Gang Busters* (1942), *Junior G-Men of the Air* (1942) and *Overland Trail* (1942).

Robert F. Hill's other serial credits include *The Flaming Disc* (Universal, 1920), *The Adventures of Tarzan* (Weiss Bros., 1921), *The Adventures of Robinson Crusoe* (Universal, 1922), *The Radio King* (Universal, 1922), *The Social Buccaneer* (Universal, 1922), *The Phantom Fortune* (Universal, 1922), *Idaho* (Pathe, 1925), *Wild West* (Pathe, 1925), *The Bar-C Mystery* (Pathe, 1926), *The Return of the Riddle Rider* (Universal, 1927), *Blake of Scotland Yard* (Universal, 1927), *Haunted Island* (Universal, 1928), *Spell of the Circus* (Universal, 1931), *Tarzan the Fearless* (Principal, 1933), *Queen of the Jungle* (Screen Attractions, (1935), *Shadow of Chinatown* (Victory, 1936), and *Blake of Scotland Yard* (Victory, 1937).

······················

Chapter 2: "The Living Dead"

Synopsis

As Ming and Azura watch on a televisor, Zarkov's rocketship is thrown out of control, spinning into a crash dive. Leaving the laboratory, Ming sees a piece of machinery that has fallen off Zarkov's rocketship and knows that Flash Gordon has arrived on Mars. Aware that Flash and Zarkov will attempt to destroy the nitron lamp and save the Earth, Ming and Azura board a Martian stratosled with a group of Azura's soldiers and set out in search of the Earth people.

Zarkov's ship, crippled beyond repair, has crashed in the Valley of Desolation. Dale sees the approaching stratosled, and, aware that the occupants are likely to be enemies, Flash, Zarkov, Happy and Dale hide behind nearby boulders. Using the stratosled's searchlight, Ming sees Zarkov's disabled rocketship in the valley below and orders the stratosled to land. Ming disembarks with a search party of soldiers, leaving Azura on board.

Meanwhile, Flash, leaving the others safely hidden in the rocks, stealthily approaches the Martian stratosled. After a brief struggle in which he overpowers the soldiers left to guard the ship, he enters and encounters Queen Azura, who immediately disappears by using her magic powers. Flash orders the stratosled pilot to blast off and land near the area where he had left Zarkov, Dale and Happy. As the stratosled gains altitude, Flash sees Ming in the valley below. The stratosled lands, picking up Zarkov, Dale and Happy. When Flash tells them that Ming is still alive, Zarkov realizes that Ming is the evil genius behind the attempted destruction of Earth. Under Flash's orders, the Martian pilot flies the stratosled toward the nitron lamp. The pilot attempts to retake control of the stratosled with a Martian raygun. Flash overpowers him, but the Martian breaks free and escapes from the ship, parachuting to the ground with a Martian "batwing" flying cape he is wearing.

Zarkov takes control of the stratosled, and they continue on toward the nitron lamp, planning to destroy it with a blast from a nitron raygun left behind by the pilot. Sighting their ship as it approaches the nitron lamp, a death squadron of Martian stratosleds blasts off to intercept them. In the air battle that follows, Flash manages to shoot down one Martian stratosled, but their ship is badly damaged in the dogfight.

Ming has now returned to the palace, and he and Azura, contacting the Martian flight commander by televisor, determine that Zarkov's disabled stratosled will land near the kingdom of the Clay People in the Valley of Desolation. Azura orders her soldiers to follow the Earth people, despite the fact that entering the kingdom of the Clay People will almost certainly mean their death.

Zarkov's disabled stratosled lands in the valley, and the Earth people disembark, pursued by arriving Martian soldiers. Holding the Martians off by causing an avalanche with a nitron gun blast, Flash, Zarkov, Dale and Happy retreat into a nearby cave. Dale sees something move against the cave wall and screams as she sees a man emerge from the rock. Slowly, the dreaded Clay People materialize from the cavern walls, pursuing Flash and his friends. When Happy tries to stop them with a gun, it proves ineffective, with the Clay People only laughing at the bullets. The Clay People force them into an alcove, where the rocky ceiling, controlled by a hidden mechanism, slowly descends, threatening to crush the Earth people...

Flash and his friends enter the kingdom of the Clay People. From left: Frank Shannon, Donald Kerr, Jean Rogers, Buster Crabbe.

Comments

Chapter 2 introduces the memorable Clay People, with their king played by C. Montague Shaw (1882–1968), a veteran actor who was a familiar presence in serials, appearing in chapterplays like *Undersea Kingdom* (Republic, 1936) and *Zorro's Fighting Legion* (Republic, 1939). According to studio documents, the Clay People were originally called "the Shadow People" in an early script draft.

The special effects in chapter 2 are indicative of the technical work's overall quality throughout the serial — a mixture of the imaginative and the tacky. The takeoff of Queen Azura's death squadron, with the fleet of stratosleds blasting off and gaining altitude in a graceful circular pattern, is well-done; but the shot of the Martian spaceport is incredibly cheap, even by serial standards, and Flash's downing of a Martian stratosled — by firing at it from the porthole of another ship with a conventional *six-shooter*— must surely be one of the most outrageously unbelievable scenes in film history. Still, even when this serial fails to convince, it remains enjoyable and moves along at a steady, rapid pace, gliding over the many technical rough spots.

....

Chapter 3: "Queen of Magic"

Synopsis

As Flash, Dale, Zarkov and Happy are about to be crushed by the descending rocks, Flash blasts a hole in the cavern wall with a raygun, and they escape into the corridor beyond. Queen Azura's soldiers are following Flash's party but are ambushed by the Clay People, who steal their weapons. The Martian soldiers continue on in pursuit of Flash and his friends, and when they attack the Earth people, the soldiers are driven off in the ensuing fight. Flash, Dale, Zarkov and Happy are then overcome by gas injected into the cave, and lose consciousness as the Clay People close in upon them.

Later, Flash awakens in a large cave chamber to find that he is now dressed in the uniform of Queen Azura's death squadron, and he sees that Dale, Zarkov and Happy, who are also reviving, are dressed in Martian clothing as well. Flash's movements interrupt a light beam, which sends a signal, and the Clay King, followed by a retinue of his subjects, enters the chamber. The Clay King tells Flash that they had initially mistaken the Earth people for Azura's soldiers, but realized this was untrue when they saw Flash and his friends fighting the Martians. Flash tells the Clay People that he and his friends have come from Earth to stop Ming and Azura from destroying the world with the nitron lamp. The Clay King replies that he and his people are unable to help Flash in his mission; a once-powerful race, the Clay People have been reduced to outcasts by the vengeful Azura's magic and banished to the Valley of Desolation.

The Clay King demands that Flash help them in their planned revolt against Azura, and in their quest to regain their normal bodies and dispel Azura's curse by stealing the magic jewel she wears. To this end, the Clay People have provided the Martian clothing that Flash and his friends now wear, in order to aid them in entering Azura's palace undetected. To insure Flash's cooperation, the Clay King insists that Dale and Happy remain behind in the caverns as hostages. Flash reluctantly agrees.

Flash (Buster Crabbe, center) and his friends are captured by the Clay People. This still shows art director Ralph DeLacey's low-budget set design to good advantage.

Flash and Zarkov leave the cavern and board a Martian stratosled, but a Martian soldier left behind by the death squadron, hiding nearby, sees them. As Flash and Zarkov blast off, the Martian soldier follows them in another stratosled. *The pursuing Martian tries to shoot them down in a mid-air battle, but is blasted out of the sky by Flash and Zarkov, the stratosled crashing in the mountains below.* (Note: The scene described here in italics, containing about 90 seconds of footage, is missing from the DVD of *Flash Gordon's Trip to Mars* distributed by Image Entertainment. The scene *was* present in the 16mm prints of the serial distributed to television in the 1970s and 1980s.)

Flash and Zarkov are almost detected as they approach Queen Azura's city by a televisor aboard the stratosled, but they disable the machine and continue on to Azura's palace. Landing near the palace, Flash disguises himself with a Martian helmet and flight goggles, and, pretending that he is a death squadron soldier who has captured Zarkov, is escorted across a light bridge to Azura's throne room.

In the powerhouse laboratory, Tarnak, a duplicitous subject of Azura's who is really loyal to Ming, hears of Azura's meeting with the death squadron pilot (Flash in disguise) and informs Ming that an Earthman has been captured. Flash and Zarkov are granted an audience before Queen Azura, and as Flash, still posing as her soldier, tells her that the rest of the Earth people have remained in the Clay Kingdom, he sees Azura's hand touch a jewel about her neck at the mention of her hated enemies. Realizing that this must be the jewel that can lift the curse from the Clay People, Flash reveals his true identity and, tearing the jewel from Azura's bosom, flees the palace with Zarkov, taking Azura along as a prisoner.

Ming has secretly watched this, and as Flash and Zarkov leave the palace with Azura, Ming returns to the laboratory and conspires with Tarnak to open fire on the landing tower and destroy it with a powerful oscillator before Flash and Zarkov can escape in a stratosled. Aware that Queen Azura will be killed in the destruction, and that his master Ming will take her place as ruler of Mars, Tarnak agrees, and the power in the laboratory increases as the oscillator's energy is focused on the landing tower. Before Flash and Zarkov can reach the landing tower with Azura, the platform begins to tremble and fall apart, disintegrating as it bursts into flame...

Comments

The scene of Flash and Zarkov being led across a Martian "light bridge" by a death squadron soldier (familiar character actor Kenneth Duncan) includes an impressive backdrop painting of Queen Azura's city, which was added to the scene by rear projection. The

The Clay King delivers an ultimatum to Flash. From left: C. Montague Shaw (gesturing), Buster Crabbe, Frank Shannon, Jean Rogers, Donald Kerr.

sequence also contains some amusing dialogue: when Zarkov, unfamiliar with the light bridge, balks at walking across it, death squadron soldier Duncan remarks to Flash (in disguise as another soldier), "These Earth men must be a stupid lot. He's evidently never seen a light bridge before!" Intentionally funny throwaway dialogue like this is one of the pleasures of Universal and Columbia serials; Republic took their own bland and overrated serials far too seriously to inject humor of this sort.

More props, costumes and footage from the first serial continue to pop up in chapter 3. One of the servant girls in Queen Azura's palace throne room wears a costume worn by Priscilla Lawson in the first serial. A clip of King Kala's undersea Shark City is inexplicably used to represent Azura's Martian city at one point (this blunder was corrected with a new — and more convincing — miniature of Azura's city inserted in the feature version, *Mars Attacks the World*), and a clip of King Vultan's sky city from the first serial, bursting into flame, is intercut when the landing tower is destroyed.

······················

Chapter 4: "Ancient Enemies"

Synopsis

As the landing tower crumbles, Ming watches on the televisor as Flash saves himself and Azura by swinging from the falling structure on a loose cable. On the ground below, Flash discovers Zarkov, half-buried in rubble but still alive. As he tries to help Zarkov, Azura opens a hidden compartment in her ring and blows a cloud of powder at Flash, who loses consciousness when he breathes it. Azura's soldiers arrive, taking Flash and Zarkov to Azura's throne room.

Azura, impressed by Flash's bravery, attempts to persuade him to join her as an ally. Flash refuses, condemning Azura and Ming for their attempted destruction of the Earth, and Ming, enraged by Flash's defiance, calls for Flash and Zarkov to be executed.

Ming, with a contingency of death squadron soldiers, escorts Flash and Zarkov out of the palace and orders them to climb a ladder to the top of the nitron lamp platform, where they will be killed by the white-hot lamp beam. But Flash, overpowering one Martian soldier, takes a raygun and kills another. Cornered at the top of the lamp platform, Flash and Zarkov are free but can't escape from the lamp, so to create a diversion they cut through a nearby fuel pipe with a raygun blast, causing flame to erupt from the pipe, driving back Ming and his soldiers. Flash leaps from the lamp, with Zarkov joining him. Holding a raygun on Ming, they force him into the powerhouse laboratory and demand that he turn over the supply of nitron to them.

As Ming attempts to show them where the nitron is by using a televisor, a fuel pipe in the lab explodes, spewing flame. Ming, his robes fireproof, walks through the fire unharmed and opens the laboratory door, letting the Martian soldiers into the lab. Flash and Zarkov flee the lab, but the soldiers are unable to follow because of the burning fuel pipe. Ming shuts off the flame, and the soldiers enter the lab, but Flash and Zarkov have escaped.

Near the Martian airdrome, Flash and Zarkov see one of Queen Azura's stratosleds taking off with a supply of nitron to bomb the Clay People. They steal another stratosled and follow the bomber.

In the caves of the Clay Kingdom, the Clay King tells an anxious Dale and Happy that his informants have told him that Flash has betrayed the Clay People by saving Azura's life. Dale and Happy know that there must be some sort of misunderstanding and tell the Clay King so. In response, the Clay King, aware that Queen Azura's bomber squadron is approaching, orders Dale and Happy to be chained at the mouth of the cavern, where they will be the first to die if the Clay People are bombed.

Queen Azura's death squadron ship appears in the sky above and drops a series of bombs that explode progressively closer to the helpless Dale and Happy. Arriving in their stratosled, Flash and Zarkov see this and engage Queen Azura's bomber in a dogfight. They are unable to shoot the other craft down since it is protected by armor, and Flash orders Zarkov to bail out, using a Martian batwing cape. As Zarkov does so, Flash steers the stratosled directly at the Martian bomber, planning to bail out before the ships collide; but the door jams before Flash can escape, and the stratosleds crash together in a cataclysmic explosion...

Comments

The exterior of the nitron lamp platform was actually the outside of the water tank in which Flash fought King Kala's octosac in the first serial. The powerhouse laboratory — a huge room full of futuristic machinery and crackling electrical devices — was one of art director Ralph DeLacey's most impressive sets, and the film's most expensive, costing $4,780.

There is a noticeable continuity error in this episode. When Ming, wearing his fireproof robes, walks through the laboratory fire, Flash comments to Zarkov, "That's the way he tricked us before!" in an apparent reference to Ming's demise at the conclusion of the first serial. This, despite the fact that in the first serial Ming was simply enveloped by mist as he sacrificed himself to the Great God Tao, not consumed by fire. Note also that this intentionally ambiguous "death" was observed by neither Flash, Zarkov, nor anyone else besides Ming's high priest!

. . . .

Chapter 5: "The Boomerang"

Synopsis

Flash bails out of the Martian stratosled, using a batwing cape, just before the ships collide and explode. Landing safely, he reunites with Zarkov. Still chained to the cavern opening, Dale and Happy see this, but they are forced back into the cave by the Clay People.

Flash and Zarkov enter the cavern, where they see a bizarre subterranean tube conveyance outside the Clay King's chamber. Spying on the Clay King, they overhear as Dale and Happy are told that if they are forced to spend another day in the caves, they will be transformed into clay themselves. Zarkov deduces that there must be something about the cavern atmosphere that transforms people into clay; he and Flash decide that they must obtain a supply of nitron from Queen Azura's laboratory in order to force the Clay King to release Dale and Happy.

Zarkov (Frank Shannon, left) and Flash (Buster Crabbe) reach Queen Azura's palace in a Martian subway car.

Luring a clay guard from his post, Flash and Zarkov board the tube device and, through a subway-like tunnel, travel to a secret alcove leading to Queen Azura's laboratory. Climbing a ladder to the lab, Flash and Zarkov enter and fight with several Martian soldiers and Ming's assistant Tarnak, who they overpower. Zarkov questions Tarnak, and they learn that there is almost no nitron available — they will have to keep the nitron beam in operation instead of destroying it in order to produce more nitron, with which Zarkov plans to invent a radioactive weapon to force Dale and Happy's release from the Clay People.

Ming and Azura hear this over the televisor, and Azura, wanting this powerful new weapon for her own use, orders her soldiers to surround the laboratory. Flash and Zarkov hear the activated televisor in the laboratory, and Flash, realizing they have been overheard, correctly assumes that soldiers are on the way. Leaving the laboratory while Zarkov works, Flash decoys the soldiers away from the lab and locks them in a nearby room.

In the powerhouse laboratory, Zarkov invents a paralyzer gun, using the small amount of nitron remaining in the lab. At Flash's suggestion, he tests the ray on Flash, who is completely paralyzed when the ray strikes him.

In the corridor outside the lab, Ming and Azura arrive, and Ming frees the soldiers imprisoned by Flash, destroying the locked door with a raygun blast. Ming and Azura stealthily enter the laboratory, and their soldiers capture Zarkov as Flash stands helplessly paralyzed by the effects of the ray.

As Zarkov works in the laboratory, Flash (Buster Crabbe, top) decoys the Martian soldiers.

Zarkov tells Ming that if the power cells in the paralyzer ray are not removed imme-diately, the device will explode. Ming allows Zarkov to remove the cells, which reverses the flow of energy through the ray machine and revives Flash, who pretends that he is still paralyzed. Springing into action, Flash takes Ming by surprise. Turning the ray on Ming and the soldiers, he paralyzes them — just as Azura escapes by magically disappearing. Flash and Zarkov find that they are unable to use the tunnel because it has been filled with poi-son gas by Ming and Azura, and try to return to the Clay Kingdom on foot.

Meanwhile, Azura has reappeared in her throne room and ordered a bombing raid against the Clay People. A death squadron bomber sees Flash and Zarkov on the ground below as they approach the Clay Kingdom. Breaking formation, it descends and fires on them. Zarkov is injured by a ray blast from the bomber. Flash leaves the paralyzer raygun on a nearby rock as he goes to help the fallen Zarkov. But Flash has accidentally tripped the mechanism, and when he crosses the beam he is paralyzed. The death squadron bomber crew sees this, and as Flash stands motionless and helpless in the paralyzer beam, they fly low above the ground, planning to run Flash down with the stratosled.

Comments

The underground Martian "subway" tube leading from the Clay Kingdom to Queen Azura's palace is one of this serial's more ingenious gimmicks; while the ending of this chapter has to be one of the most unbelievable in the entire serial — for the approaching stratosled to run Flash down, it would have to be skimming over the rocky terrain at an altitude of about 3 feet!

Although most of Doctor Zarkov's "scientific" comments are near-meaningless techno-babble (as previously mentioned, there is far more fantasy than science in these films), he does correctly state in this episode that Mars is 40 million miles from Earth (at least *approximately*, and at the closest point of its orbit).

The paralyzer gun invented by Zarkov had been seen before in the 1934 Universal serial *The Vanishing Shadow*, starring Onslow Stevens.

....

Chapter 6: "Tree-Men of Mars"

Synopsis

Zarkov recovers and manages to shove the paralyzed Flash to the ground, out of harm's way, as the stratosled bomber draws near. Missing their intended target, the bomber crew loses control of their ship and crashes into the nearby hills. Reversing the polarity of the ray machine, Zarkov releases Flash from his paralysis just as the Martian soldiers emerge from the wrecked stratosled. Flash pretends he is still paralyzed until they approach. Flash suddenly leaps into action, fighting the soldiers, with Zarkov paralyzing one of the Mar-tians aiming a raygun at Flash.

Flash, propping up an unconscious Martian soldier, hides behind him and calls for help, tricking the remaining death squadron soldiers into approaching so that he and Zarkov can overpower them in a fight. Determining that the stratosled is irreparably disabled, Flash and Zarkov realize that they will be unable to travel through the underground tube since it is filled with lethal gas. They decide to return to the powerhouse laboratory to obtain gas masks.

Donning Martian batwing capes found in the stratosled, they leap off a nearby cliff and fly back to the laboratory. Stealthily entering, they see Ming and the soldiers reviving from the paralyzer ray's effects. Holding Ming off with the paralyzer, they find the gas masks and enter the doorway leading to the gas-filled subterranean tunnel, with Ming's soldiers following them after Queen Azura magically appears in the laboratory.

The soldiers report the existence of the underground tube to Azura. She and Ming realize that the underground tube must lead to the Clay Kingdom, and Azura, using her magic powers, transforms two of her reluctant soldiers into clay men so that they can follow Flash and Zarkov.

Flash and Zarkov arrive in the Clay Kingdom and, entering the Clay King's chamber, paralyze two of his guards, planning to release Dale and Happy from their cavern cell. They threaten the Clay King with the same fate if they aren't released, and, as Zarkov holds the paralyzer gun on the Clay King, he agrees. The newly-created Clay Men sent by Azura arrive and, approaching Zarkov from behind, seize the paralyzer ray. Flash, having gone into the cavern cell to free Dale and Happy, sees this and, with a well-aimed rock, knocks

Returning to the Clay Kingdom, Flash (Buster Crabbe) and Zarkov (Frank Shannon) are observed by one of the Clay Men.

Flash and his friends are trapped by the Forest People in *Flash Gordon's Trip to Mars*, chapter 6. From left: Frank Shannon, Donald Kerr, Buster Crabbe, Jean Rogers.

the paralyzer from the hand of the clay man. Both of Azura's clay men flee, but the paralyzer gun has been smashed on the cavern floor and is now useless.

Flash tells the Clay King that he should have trusted them, and after Flash tells the Clay King of their former encounter with Ming on Mongo, the Clay King realizes that the Earth people are his friends and advises them to seek out the Forest People for assistance in their struggle against Ming and Azura.

At the palace, Queen Azura's clay men, their normal bodies restored, admit their failure, and Azura punishes them by transforming them into clay permanently, banishing them forever to the Clay Kingdom. On the televisor, Azura and Ming watch as Flash and his friends approach a shrine in the Forest Kingdom. Unaware that they are also being watched by the Forest People, Happy uses his camera to take a picture of the idol. From afar, Azura uses her magic to disintegrate the idol, and the enraged Forest People, believing that Happy has destroyed their idol with his camera, emerge from hiding and attack the Earth people. As the Forest People shoot flaming arrows at them, a fire erupts at the base of a huge tree, and Flash, Dale, Zarkov and Happy are surrounded by encroaching flames...

Comments

Chapter 6 is the first episode containing a flashback to events from the first serial, using clips from *Flash Gordon* chapter 1, as well as footage from the invisibility sequence later in the serial. This technique, used to pad the sequel serial, was utilized several times in *Trip to Mars* from this point onward, and results in a continuity disruption since Jean Rogers was blonde in the first serial (the laboratory cost for dupe negatives of *Flash Gordon* scenes was $300).

Speaking of continuity, there is a noticeable error in the chapter 6 dialogue: As Flash and his friends enter the Forest Kingdom, they are observed by Ming and Azura on the televisor, with Ming commenting, "What if the Fire People accept them as friends?" prompting Azura to destroy the idol to insure that the Earth people will be attacked. *Fire People? Who* are the *Fire People?* Ming is obviously referring to the *Forest People*, but Charles Middleton says *Fire People* not once, but *twice* in this scene, and the error is even repeated in the chapter 7 recap footage. Why this obvious script error wasn't caught and fixed, either on the set while it was being shot or in post production, is anyone's guess.

The set for the Forest Kingdom, shot outdoors on the backlot in front of a painted cyclorama, is another example of Ralph DeLacey's fine art direction. The cost for this set was $1,900.

....

Chapter 7: "The Prisoner of Mongo"

Synopsis

As they are attacked by the Forest People, Flash places Dale, who has fainted, inside the hollow of a nearby tree for protection. When he helps Zarkov and Happy inside the huge tree base after they are overcome by the flames and smoke, Flash sees that Dale has vanished. As they search for her, they are attacked by a horde of Forest People and taken through an underground lair below the tree's root system. They are escorted into the chamber of Mighty Toran, ruler of the Forest People, where they are reunited with Dale.

Angry that the idol has been destroyed, Toran blames the Earth people, despite Flash's attempts to explain, and consigns them to an underground death cell. Toran orders Captain Rama to communicate with Ming, telling him that the Forest People have captured the Earth people. This news is relayed to Ming's assistant, Tarnak, who informs Ming. Ming immediately sends death squadron soldiers to the Forest Kingdom.

Meanwhile, Flash, Dale, Zarkov and Happy, anxiously awaiting their fate in the death cell, notice menacing smoke emanating from the cavern wall. At first they think they are being subjected to poison gas, but suddenly the rock wall crumbles and Prince Barin, their friend from the planet Mongo, crawls through the opening.

Barin tells his friends that he had flown to Mars to enlist the Forest People in his struggle against Ming, but they turned on him and imprisoned him in a neighboring cell. When Barin learned that Earth people had been captured, he realized that Flash was on Mars, and used a vial of amputrol acid to dissolve the wall between their cells. Barin tells them that a black sapphire displayed in a shrine at the temple of Kalu, located nearby, can nullify the magical white jewel that gives Queen Azura her powers.

Top: The Earth people are confined to a subterranean cell in chapter 7 of *Flash Gordon's Trip to Mars.* From left: Frank Shannon, Buster Crabbe, Donald Kerr, Jean Rogers. *Bottom:* Rejoining their friend Prince Barin, Flash and his friends escape from the Forest People. From left: Buster Crabbe, Jean Rogers, Frank Shannon, Donald Kerr, Richard Alexander.

Flash (Buster Crabbe) battles the Forest People.

When the Forest People guards return to the death cell to bring food to the prisoners, Flash, Barin, Zarkov and Happy ambush them, and escape with Dale. Led by Prince Barin, they leave the huge tree and walk to the temple of Kalu, where Flash leaves Dale and Happy in the nearby forest. Approaching the temple, Flash climbs a nearby tree, planning to swing into the shrine from above and take the black sapphire.

Dale and Happy, undercover in the forest, see a Martian stratosled land nearby, and watch as Azura's soldiers emerge and confer with Captain Rama, who tells them that the Earth people have escaped. Leaving Dale, Happy runs to inform Flash. Meanwhile, Flash battles a tree man in the branches above the temple, and falls from the tree to the ground as he is attacked by the Forest People. A tree man aims a heat ray at Flash, and as he lies helpless on the ground, Flash is slowly burned alive...

Comments

Mighty Toran of the forest people was played by Anthony Warde, who would play Killer Kane, the chief nemesis of *Buck Rogers* (Buster Crabbe) in the Universal serial released the following year.

A rather obvious double stands in for Frank Shannon (Zarkov) in the underground fight seen inside the tree. Photos of the stunt double were used for at least one theatrical poster.

....

Chapter 8: "The Black Sapphire of Kalu"

Synopsis

As Flash writhes in agony on the ground in the path of the heat ray, Dale stealthily boards a Martian stratosled and blasts off. Happy suddenly arrives and, seeing Flash's predicament, shoots the tree-man holding the ray on Flash. Flash recovers and heads for the temple of Kalu as Zarkov and Barin arrive and more Forest People attack.

High above in the stratosled, Dale drops a bomb that wipes out many of the attacking Forest People. Flash, Zarkov and Barin enter the temple and fight a horde of Forest People, finally locating the black sapphire of Kalu. With the black sapphire finally in Flash's possession, they battle their way out of the temple and reunite with Happy, who holds off the remaining tree-men with a nitron gun. The magical black sapphire will now protect Flash and all of his friends from Azura's spells.

As they depart from the temple, a tree-man in the branches overhead watches them and shoots Happy with a metallic arrow. Although badly wounded, Happy manages to

In the Forest Kingdom. From left: Buster Crabbe, Jean Rogers, Donald Kerr.

Flash (Buster Crabbe, center) and Barin (Richard Alexander), back in the Clay Kingdom for chapter 8 of *Flash Gordon's Trip to Mars*.

stagger after his friends, who are unaware of his injury. Flash, Barin and Zarkov watch as the stratosled descends and lands, and are surprised when Dale emerges to join them. Then they see that Happy, who has collapsed in pain, has been hurt. Carrying Happy to the stratosled, they fly back to the Clay Kingdom. In the caves of the Clay People, the Clay King has Happy placed in a special chamber that fills with healing vapors, which will hasten his recovery. Flash reveals that they now have the black sapphire, and that after they destroy the nitron lamp, they will force Azura to come to the Clay People and lift her curse. Zarkov stays behind in the Clay Kingdom with Dale to supervise Happy's recovery, as Flash and Barin use the underground tube system to reach Azura's palace.

Flash and Barin enter the palace behind Queen Azura's throne where Azura holds court. As a subject reports on the Earth people, Flash and Barin suddenly emerge from behind the throne, defiantly confronting her. When she tries to retaliate with her magic, Azura is stunned to find that she is powerless. Flash reveals that he now has the black sapphire. Flash tells Barin to escort Azura to the Clay People, and as they leave, he remains behind to destroy the nitron lamp.

In the laboratory, a technician, Sandor, reports to Ming that the nitron being drawn from the Earth is not as pure as previous extracts, and Ming deduces that the Earth's air supply is near exhaustion. Ming's assistant Tarnak then arrives and tells Ming that Flash now has the black sapphire, and that Flash and Barin have captured Queen Azura.

Meanwhile, Flash warily makes his way through the city, intent on destroying the nitron lamp. He overpowers a Martian soldier, and is fired on by another soldier. Escaping, he finally reaches the powerhouse lab, but Ming and Tarnak are waiting to ambush him. Tarnak allows himself to be captured by Flash, and when Flash demands that the nitron lamp be turned off, Tarnak leads Flash to a generator room, knocks him out, and locks Flash inside. Ming then turns on the generator room power full blast, laughing maniacally as a lethal shower of electrical sparks rains down on Flash...

Comments

Chapter 8 presented Jean Rogers with one of her few strong scenes in the serial, as she flies the stratosled over the Forest Kingdom, dropping bombs. Although she had been showcased in the first serial, where her physical attributes were fully exploited, she was, except for a couple of episodes, consigned to the periphery of *Trip to Mars*.

A technical flub in chapter 8 occurs when Tarnak leads Flash into the generator room — the clearly visible shadow of a studio microphone can be seen on the wall behind Flash.

Dale (Jean Rogers) and Happy (Donald Kerr) watch from cover as a Martian stratosled lands.

. . . .

Chapter 9: "Symbol of Death"

Synopsis

Staggering to his feet, Flash begins to recover from the blow dealt by Tarnak as he is showered with electrical sparks. Grabbing his nitron gun off the floor, Flash blasts a hole in the side of the wall and escapes into the city outside. Ming, sure that Flash is dead, enters the generator room to recover the black sapphire and is shocked to discover that Flash has escaped. He angrily orders Tarnak to call out the city guards and search for the Earthman.

In the city, Flash sees a platoon of guards and overpowers a lone guard. Disguising himself in the guard's uniform, he passes the sentries unnoticed, crosses the light bridge to the airdrome platform, and, gaining control of a huge ray cannon after using his nitron gun on the guards, aims the ray cannon at the nitron lamp, damaging it severely. Ming sees the nitron lamp being destroyed and orders his guards to fire on the airdrome platform. Flash, knocked unconscious by the blast, is captured by guards and delivered to Tarnak, who takes the black sapphire from Flash and places it in a metal box made of nutrinium, which nullifies the jewel's magic power.

Queen Azura regains her magic powers and escapes from the Earth people. From left: Richard Alexander, Jean Rogers, Frank Shannon, C. Montague Shaw (seated), Donald Kerr, Beatrice Roberts.

Meanwhile, Barin has arrived in the Clay Kingdom with the captured Queen Azura, and the Clay King demands that Azura release his people from her curse. Azura agrees, and Barin releases her hands from her bonds so that she can make the appropriate magical gestures. But Azura suddenly extends her hands upward and, calling upon her magic powers, abruptly disappears. Seeing that Azura's powers have been restored, Zarkov and Barin realize that something must have happened to Flash and the black sapphire. They leave in a stratosled to rescue Flash.

Flash, in chains, is brought before Ming. When Ming boasts that he will continue his efforts to destroy the Earth, Flash attacks him, but is subdued by his captors and taken away to await execution.

With the nitron lamp disabled by Flash, the powerful storms wreaking havoc on Earth have ceased, and the conclave of scientists meeting in Washington to analyze the disasters conclude that Flash Gordon and Doctor Zarkov must be responsible.

On Mars, Zarkov and Barin land the stratosled near Azura's city and search for Flash. Ming orders Tarnak to lock the black sapphire in his private vault. He plans to give Azura the metal box — empty. In the throne room, Queen Azura receives a report from one of her guards informing her that Ming has captured Flash. While Zarkov and Barin make

Ming the Merciless (Charles Middleton) communicates a threat to Flash, who is imprisoned in the Disintegrating Room.

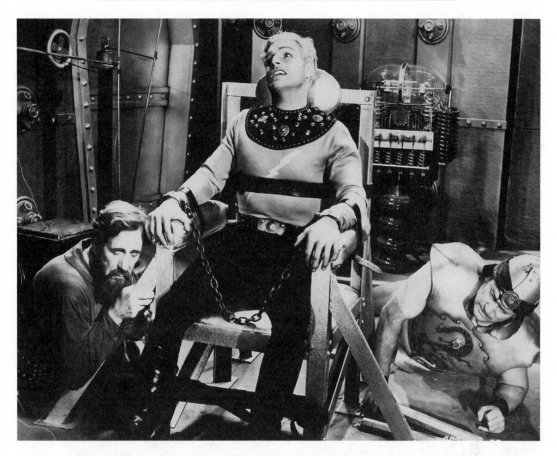

Zarkov and Barin attempt to free Flash, who is trapped in the Disintegrating Room. From left: Frank Shannon, Buster Crabbe, Richard Alexander.

their way through the city outside, Azura magically appears before Ming, who presents her with the empty metal box. Ming lies by telling her that the black sapphire has been stolen and deceitfully blaming Tarnak for allowing Flash to outwit him.

As Flash is led before Ming and Azura, Azura demands the black sapphire; Flash truthfully tells her that he doesn't know where it is. Ming orders Flash to be confined in the Disintegrating Room, where he will be executed. Relieved that Flash will soon be disposed of, and believing that then no one will know the location of the black sapphire, the trusting Azura thanks Ming for his loyalty and magically disappears. As soon as she is gone, Ming orders Tarnak to communicate with Mighty Toran, monarch of the Forest People, and tell him that he now has the black sapphire — to use against Azura.

Shortly thereafter, Zarkov and Barin kidnap Tarnak and force him to reveal that Flash is being held in the powerhouse Disintegrating Room. In the disintegrating room Flash is strapped to a chair, while Ming, communicating from a control room over a loudspeaker, demonstrates the power of his death ray by destroying a nearby statue made of "the hardest metal on Mars."

As the statue crumbles to dust before Flash's eyes, Zarkov and Barin are on the powerhouse roof above, trying to force open a skylight. They are spotted by Martian gun crew

11 on the airdrome platform, and the Martians fire on them with a ray cannon. Blown through the roof by the explosion, they fall into the Disintegrating Room just as Ming's death ray falls upon first Barin and Zarkov, then Flash...

Comments

Chapter 9 contains another of Eddie Keyes' inventive "live" special effects — a repeat of the crumbling statue gag previously used in chapter 6, with the "disintegration" effect augmented by an optically superimposed "death ray." This episode also presents one of the serial's most outrageous plot devices: When Zarkov and Barin attempt to gain entry to the Disintegrating Room through a skylight and encounter difficulty, Barin nonchalantly reaches out of camera range and produces a convenient crowbar!

....

Chapter 10: "Incense of Forgetfulness"

Synopsis

Escaping from his bonds, Flash evades the ray and climbs upward through the open

Dale (Jean Rogers, center) is abducted by the Forest People.

Her will and memory destroyed by the Incense of Forgetfulness, Dale (Jean Rogers) is brought before Mighty Toran (Anthony Warde), the forest monarch.

skylight. Reaching down, he helps Barin and Zarkov to the roof above. Ming learns that the Earth people have escaped; but with the powerhouse surrounded by guards, Flash, Zarkov and Barin are trapped on the roof above. Desperate to escape before they are spotted, they climb down a ladder leading back into the powerhouse, emerging in a corridor just as guards arrive on the roof. Forced to go forward through the powerhouse, they are attacked by more guards in the corridor. During the fight that follows, Flash draws some of the guards away and locks them in a nearby room.

Flash, Zarkov and Barin board their stratosled and return to the Clay Kingdom, rejoining Dale and Happy. Flash tells them that the nitron lamp has been disabled, and that he is sure Ming has possession of the black sapphire. The Clay King is dejected that Flash has lost the jewel, but Flash promises the Clay King that he will not consider his mission on Mars fully accomplished until Azura's curse has been lifted from the Clay People.

Barin suggests that they search for the rocketship in which he traveled from Mongo to Mars, since that will give them a much better chance to recapture Azura. In the palace throne room, Ming reports to Azura that Flash and his friends are headed toward the Forest Kingdom, and Azura demands that the Earth people be stopped.

The stratosled lands in the Forest Kingdom, with Flash, Dale, Zarkov, Barin and Happy disembarking and splitting up to look for Barin's rocketship. Barin and Zarkov search in one direction, while Flash, Dale and Happy search in another. Flash then leaves Dale and Happy, who are attacked by tree-men. Happy is overpowered in the fight, and Dale is kidnapped by the Forest People, who take her to the temple of Kalu. There, the temple priest forces Dale to stand in the "Incense of Forgetfulness," and she is compelled to recite an oath of loyalty to Kalu as her memory and willpower fade.

Meanwhile, Happy has told Zarkov and Barin about Dale, and they hurry to meet Flash, who then tries to sneak into the temple while Zarkov, Barin and Happy wait outside. As Flash battles the Forest People in the temple, Dale, completely mesmerized and bound by an oath of loyalty to Kalu, picks up a dagger and stabs Flash in the back...

Comments

For younger viewers at the time, seeing Dale Arden stab Flash Gordon (in the back, no less) must have been a traumatic experience! This is one of the serial's best episodes, despite the fact that Prince Barin's insistence on retrieving his rocketship so that he and Flash stand a "better chance" of recapturing Queen Azura makes very little sense (they already have a stratosled), and seems to have been injected merely to justify a return to the Forest Kingdom.

Another flashback to the first serial, covering the "Tournament of Death" events in chapter 8 of *Flash Gordon*, is intercut here to explain Barin's loyalty to the Earth people in their struggle against Ming.

....

Chapter 11: "Human Bait"

Synopsis

Flash collapses as Dale stabs him, and the Forest People take Dale to their king, Mighty Toran. After Zarkov, Barin and Happy take Flash away from the temple of Kalu, Zarkov determines that the knife wound is not that serious and treats Flash's injury. As the hypnotized Dale, staring blankly, is brought before Toran, the forest monarch orders his men to contact Ming and inform him that the Earth woman has been captured.

Ming, enraged that the nitron lamp is inoperative, receives Toran's message about Dale's capture and sends Martian soldiers to bring Dale to him for use as a lure in trapping Flash.

As Dale, mesmerized, is led into the stratosled, Flash, Zarkov, Barin and Happy see it blast off for Queen Azura's city, unaware that Dale is aboard. Zarkov theorizes that Dale must have been under the influence of a powerful drug when she attacked Flash. Zarkov, Flash, Barin and Happy return to the temple of Kalu, where Zarkov discovers a supply of lethium, a drug that robs people of their will. Determining that the lethium was used on Dale, they force the temple priest, under threat of exposure to the lethium mist, to admit that Dale is in the palace with Ming, and that Barin's rocketship is nearby in the Vale of Pines.

Finding the rocketship guarded by Forest People, Happy lures them away, where the tree-men are ambushed and overpowered by Flash, Barin and Zarkov. They take off in the

Queen Azura (Beatrice Roberts) and Ming the Merciless (Charles Middleton) plot against the Earth people in chapter 11 of *Flash Gordon's Trip to Mars.*

rocketship, and make plans to enter the palace and rescue Dale. En route, Zarkov reveals that the antidote to lethium is relatively simple—plain salt crystals treated with barium and nitric acid, and subjected to heat. He knows that he can find the needed materials in Ming's laboratory.

In her palace Queen Azura orders a stratosled squadron to depart at once to attack Flash and his friends, but Ming objects, revealing that he has laid a trap for Flash, who will surely come to the palace for Dale.

In the sky above, Barin's rocketship drops to an altitude of 500 metrons as Flash and Zarkov bail out in Martian batwing capes and land on the palace roof. Finding the laboratory mysteriously deserted, they enter, secretly observed by Ming. While Zarkov mixes the chemicals needed for the lethium antidote, Flash searches for Dale but cannot find her. Returning to the laboratory, Flash tunes in a Martian televisor and sees Dale being held captive in the palace. As Zarkov finishes mixing the antidote so that they can take it to Dale, he suddenly realizes that the wrong chemicals have been supplied. The mixture bubbles ominously and then erupts in a tremendous explosion...

Comments

Kane Richmond, later a serial star himself who would be featured in Republic's 1942 effort *Spy Smasher* (based on the then-popular comic book), appears in this episode as one of the Martian stratosled pilots who escorts the hypnotized Dale to Azura's palace, and would be visible in subsequent chapters of *Trip to Mars*.

The inconsistency of this serial's production quality is once again evident in chapter 11: When Flash and Zarkov fly down to the palace roof after bailing out of Barin's rocketship, they are backed by an excellent painting of the futuristic Martian city, while a bit of ragged editing later on somehow manages to place Charles Middleton's Ming in two places at once!

The interior of Barin's rocketship, which was mounted on rockers to provide movement when it was supposedly in flight, was constructed for a cost of $590.

....

Chapter 12: "Ming the Merciless"

Synopsis

Ming's assistant Tarnak enters the laboratory after the explosion and sees Flash and Zarkov lying on the floor, apparently killed by the explosion. They were only stunned by the blast, however, and after Tarnak activates a televisor screen and reports to Ming and Azura that the Earth men are dead, Flash and Zarkov suddenly leap up and overpower Tarnak, forcing him to divulge the whereabouts of the lethium antidote.

Leaving the laboratory with Tarnak as their prisoner, Flash and Zarkov see Ming and Azura approaching in the distance, accompanied by Martian soldiers. Finding the laboratory empty, Ming and Azura assume that Tarnak is disposing of the dead Earth men.

Flash and Zarkov enter Azura's palace with Tarnak and, after overpowering a guard, find Dale. They administer the lethium antidote and watch as she recovers her memory.

Flash struggles with Ming for possession of the black sapphire. From left: Beatrice Roberts, Buster Crabbe, Charles Middleton.

By now Ming has seen no trace of Tarnak and has grown suspicious, assuming the Earth men are still alive and probably at the palace searching for Dale. Azura magically disappears, and just as Flash, Zarkov and Dale are about to leave the palace, Azura reappears before the Earth people, allowing Tarnak to disarm Flash.

As Tarnak guards Dale and Zarkov, Flash tries to reason with Queen Azura, but Ming arrives and demands Flash's death. Azura objects, declaring that she has "other plans" for the Earthman, and when Ming tries to overrule her authority, she curtly declares that she will use her magic to control Ming. Ming then produces the black sapphire, which immediately nullifies Azura's magic power. The shocked Azura now realizes that Ming is a traitor and now has her under his control. In the resulting confusion, Flash suddenly attacks Ming and grabs the black sapphire, gaining the upper hand. Flash now plans to force Azura to lift her curse from the Clay People, but as Flash, Dale and Zarkov escort Ming and Azura across the light bridge to the landing tower so they can leave in a stratosled, Ming suddenly escapes by jumping off the light bridge and gliding to the ground in a Martian batwing cape. The Earth people continue on, and after forcing Azura to board her personal stratosled, they blast off for the Clay Kingdom.

Ming orders the death squadron to fly out and shoot down Queen Azura's stratosled.

Ming the Merciless escapes from the Earth people. From left: Frank Shannon, Buster Crabbe, Jean Rogers, Beatrice Roberts, stunt double for Charles Middleton.

When Azura's loyal pilots object, Ming, well aware that Azura's magic powers have been nullified and that she will die in the attack, tells the pilots that Azura's magic will protect her from harm. The death squadron blasts off on its mission.

On their way to the Clay Kingdom aboard the stratosled with Azura, Flash, Dale and Zarkov see Barin and Happy on the ground near Barin's rocketship, and drop a note to them explaining that they have captured Azura and that Barin and Happy should meet them in the Clay Kingdom. After waving to signal that they have received the note, Barin and Happy see the death squadron following Flash's stratosled, and are knocked unconscious when the death squadron drops a bomb that explodes near them.

In Flash's stratosled, Zarkov notices the death squadron following them, and the Earth people decide to land in the valley below to avoid the Martian soldiers. Azura, now desperate, offers to spare Flash's life if he will give her the black sapphire, but Flash refuses to even consider it. As Flash, Dale, Zarkov and Azura take cover in the rocky valley, they are bombed by the stratosled death squadron. Terrified, Azura runs away from the rocks, and Flash follows her — just as a death squadron bomb hits, catching both of them in a terrific explosion...

Comments

The infrared photography used in previous chapters reappears in this episode during the night scene showing Ming and Azura approaching the laboratory after the lethium antidote explosion.

The sexual interplay so pronounced in the first serial is hardly present at all in *Flash Gordon's Trip to Mars*; given the complicated plot of *Mars*, it would have probably seemed extraneous, anyway. Ming has almost no interest in Dale Arden in this serial, except to use her as bait to trap Flash. However, there seems to have been a last-minute attempt to inject a bit of romantic byplay, with Queen Azura seemingly becoming interested in Flash at this point (coyly mentioning her "other plans" for the Earthman when Ming calls for his death).

....

Chapter 13: "The Miracle of Magic"

Synopsis

Flash survives the death squadron bomb explosion unharmed, but Queen Azura is mortally wounded. Flash, Dale and Zarkov gather around her as she lies dying, and in her final moments she atones for her misdeeds by giving Flash the white sapphire, revealing to him that if the white and black sapphires are destroyed together, her curse on the Clay People will be lifted.

Covering the dead Azura with her cape, Flash, Dale and Zarkov, seeing that the death squadron bombers are landing, board the stratosled and fly toward the Clay Kingdom to rejoin Barin and Happy near Barin's rocketship. They go to the Clay Kingdom and inform the Clay King that Azura is dead, but that they now have both sapphires and can lift Azura's curse. Placing the magical jewels in an electrical chamber, Flash activates power

Top: Flash (Buster Crabbe) comes to the aid of Queen Azura (Beatrice Roberts), who has been mortally wounded by her own death squadron in *Flash Gordon's Trip to Mars*, chapter 13. *Bottom:* Flash delivers the black sapphire to the Clay People. From left: C. Montague Shaw, Frank Shannon, Jean Rogers, Richard Alexander, Donald Kerr, Buster Crabbe.

In chapter 13 of *Flash Gordon's Trip to Mars*, Flash prepares to destroy the black sapphire and lift the curse from the Clay People. From left: Frank Shannon, Richard Alexander, Jean Rogers, Buster Crabbe, Donald Kerr.

terminals that emit powerful arcs of electricity, disintegrating both sapphires. Slowly, as Flash and his friends watch in amazement, the Clay People begin to transform, regaining their normal human bodies.

Their joy is short-lived, however; another clay man soon arrives at the cave with news that Ming, now in control of the death squadron, has declared war on the Clay People, and is planning to enlist and arm Toran and the Forest People as allies. In the palace, Ming declares his plans to conquer and rule Mars as he watches the death squadron blast off for the Forest Kingdom. Leaving Dale with the Clay People, Flash, Zarkov, Barin and Happy take off in the stratosled for the Forest Kingdom, intent on stopping Ming.

Arriving in the Forest Kingdom, Zarkov and Happy are left at the stratosled while Flash and Barin stealthily approach Mighty Toran's grotto, finding it unguarded. They overhear as Toran, in the inner chamber, tells the Forest People to prepare for war on the Clay Kingdom as soon as Ming's stratosleds arrive. Flash and Barin follow the Forest People as they leave Toran's grotto, trying to catch them before the tree-men see Flash's stratosled. During the ensuing fight, they capture one tree-man. After Barin questions him at knifepoint, they learn that Ming's stratosleds will land at the far edge of the Forest Kingdom.

Returning to their stratosled, Flash and Barin rejoin Zarkov and Happy. Zarkov, scanning the sky with a telescope, sees Ming's death squadron approaching. As Flash, Zarkov, Barin and Happy blast off, Flash works out a plan to stop the death squadron. Gaining altitude and rising above the death squadron formation, Flash bails out in a Martian batwing cape and lands atop the gunport of a death squadron ship. When the co-pilot of the ship hears Flash land, he peers out of the gunport porthole to investigate. Flash knocks him unconscious and enters the stratosled. Flash then fights with the stratosled pilot for control of the bomber, and as they struggle, the stratosled, heavily loaded with nitron to arm the Forest People, veers out of control and flies toward a nearby mountain...

Comments

Chapter 13 eliminates the character of Queen Azura, with Beatrice Roberts giving an excellent performance in a touching death scene.

The final transformation of the Clay People, as the magic sapphires are destroyed and the clay men regain their normal bodies, is extremely well done, with great care taken in the effects work, while the triumphant score makes excellent use of Heinz Roemheld's music for *The Black Cat* (1934).

....

Chapter 14: "A Beast at Bay"

Synopsis

The stratosled co-pilot, regaining consciousness, takes control of the stratosled as Flash and the pilot continue fighting, and the co-pilot manages to pull the stratosled back into formation, avoiding a crack-up on the mountain. Drawing a raygun, Flash holds off the pilot and co-pilot, ordering them to fly the stratosled to the Valley of Desolation near the Clay Kingdom. The pilots announce their destination over a live televisor connected to the other death squadron bombers, but Flash interrupts them by destroying the televisor with his raygun. The other death squadron pilots have heard, though, and get away.

Flash takes the stratosled, with the pilot and co-pilot his prisoners, to the Clay People, aware that the one stratosled will contain enough nitron to provide at least a minimal defense for the Clay People. In the caves, the two captured Martians are brought in for questioning, and the stratosled pilot is startled to see that his brother Calgan, who had been exiled to the Clay Kingdom, has regained his normal body. Learning that Flash Gordon has lifted Azura's curse from the Clay People, the pilot realizes that Flash is not his enemy. He and the co-pilot offer to help Flash and his friends gain access to the palace to capture Ming.

Flash, Dale, Zarkov, Barin and Happy, accompanied by the two Martian pilots, blast off in a stratosled, landing near the city. The pilots, pretending that Flash, Dale and Barin are their prisoners, bypass the guards and, crossing the light bridge, enter the palace, while Zarkov and Happy go to the laboratory.

In the throne room, Ming, having achieved power through his assassination of Azura, is being crowned monarch of Mars by the assembled Martian nobility. Having gained

Top: Flash (Buster Crabbe, right) struggles with a Martian pilot (Kane Richmond) for control of a stratosled in *Flash Gordon's Trip to Mars*, chapter 14. *Bottom:* As Ming is crowned Monarch of Mars, Flash interrupts the ceremony. From left: Wheeler Oakman, Buster Crabbe, Charles Middleton.

access to a hidden alcove behind the throne, Flash suddenly emerges into the throne room, interrupting the ceremony and denouncing Ming as a murderous tyrant. When the Martians object, Prince Barin recalls his own experiences with Ming on the planet Mongo. When Flash asserts that Ming deliberately killed Azura to gain control of the throne, the Martian assembly is finally persuaded.

One of Ming's servants has secretly given Ming a raygun, though, and Ming, aware that his true nature has been exposed to the Martian nobles, suddenly leaps up and, holding the raygun on Flash, forces Flash into the alcove behind the throne. As the panel closes, the horrified Dale and Barin hear a raygun blast, followed by Ming's boast that he has killed Flash...

Comments

Chapter 14 contains the final *Mars* flashback to the first serial, covering events in chapters 7 and 8 of *Flash Gordon*.

The cliffhanger for this episode is an oddly-staged one, with Dale and Barin simply listening, as described above, while Flash, unseen behind the palace wall, is apparently executed by Ming.

....

Chapter 15: "An Eye for an Eye"

Synopsis

Inside the throne room alcove, Flash smashes the only light, plunging the room into darkness, and struggles desperately with Ming. Tarnak enters the alcove with Martian soldiers through another hidden wall panel and helps Ming escape while Flash battles the soldiers. Outside in the throne room, Barin blasts the alcove door open with a raygun. He and Dale are relieved to find Flash alive, but Ming has escaped.

Flash, now in control, orders the commander of the city troops to search the city for Ming. Death squadron bombers have been sent by Ming to attack the Clay People, and Flash orders the air marshall to stop them. But the air marshall, secretly loyal to Ming, surreptitiously interrupts the televisor transmission when he does so.

Attempting to sabotage Flash's efforts, the air marshall takes Zarkov, Happy and one of the friendly Martian pilots prisoners, intending to deliver them to Ming. In the palace, Dale sees that Ming has managed to reactivate the nitron lamp and tells Flash. Flash realizes that Ming has barricaded himself in the powerhouse laboratory, and sets out after him.

In the laboratory, Ming watches gleefully through a telescope as the nitron ray creates more havoc on Earth, with tidal waves and windstorms sweeping the globe. As Ming raves insanely of his plans for conquest, Tarnak, barricaded in the laboratory with him, finally realizes that Ming is hopelessly insane, and sneaks out of the laboratory.

Seeing that Zarkov and Happy have been taken prisoner, Flash manages to free Zarkov, Happy and the Martian pilot from a soldier loyal to the air marshall. They find Tarnak in the city after he has abandoned Ming in the powerhouse laboratory, and Tarnak offers to help them gain access to the building.

Zarkov (Frank Shannon) and Happy (Donald Kerr) are accompanied by two Martian pilots (Kane Richmond and Kenneth Duncan) in chapter 15 of *Flash Gordon's Trip to Mars*.

Ming sees them from the laboratory window and fires on them with a powerful raygun. Zarkov and Happy draw Ming's fire and try to divert his attention while Flash circles around and enters the laboratory. Ming hears Flash enter, though, and holds Flash off with the raygun. Ming is about to fire when the laboratory and the entire powerhouse trembles under a gigantic explosion. In the sky above, Prince Barin holds a raygun on the air marshal, whom he has captured, forcing him to bomb the powerhouse and destroy the nitron lamp. Ming is thrown off balance by the force of the explosion and stumbles in the confusion, with Flash gaining control of the situation.

They are interrupted by Tarnak, who has entered the laboratory. Holding a raygun on Ming, Tarnak vengefully forces Ming into the Disintegrating Room — over Flash's objections. Tarnak activates the disintegrating ray and kills Ming, as Flash watches helplessly. Barin's stratosled lands nearby, and he comes to the laboratory to tell Flash that the nitron lamp has been destroyed.

With the nitron lamp destroyed and Ming dead, the Earth people return to the Clay Kingdom. Leaving Barin on Mars to rule the Forest Kingdom, Flash Gordon, Dale Arden, Dr. Zarkov and Happy Hapgood blast off in Zarkov's rocketship and return to Earth, where they are welcomed with a massive parade held in their honor.

Flash (Buster Crabbe) forces his way into the powerhouse.

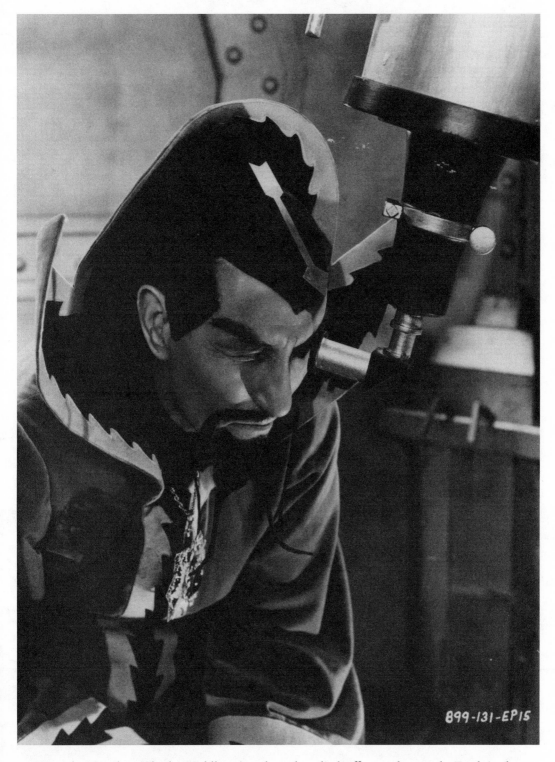

Ming the Merciless (Charles Middleton) makes a last-ditch effort to destroy the Earth in the final chapter of *Flash Gordon's Trip to Mars.*

Comments

The rather convoluted plot of *Flash Gordon's Trip to Mars* comes to an end here with a somewhat diluted wrap-up that superimposes photo portraits of the leads over the same parade footage seen in chapter 1. (Oddly, there's no portrait of Donald Kerr's Happy Hapgood character — was he arrested for stowing away aboard Zarkov's rocketship?)

The flamboyant Charles Middleton pulled out all the stops for this final episode, going irrevocably "mad" in an over-the-top performance that has to be seen to be believed.

Chapter 15's "The End" title is a specially prepared (and very well done) miniature shot of the planet Earth rapidly spinning on its axis. Oddly, this footage appears nowhere else in the serial.

Of *Flash Gordon's Trip to Mars, The Hollywood Reporter* commented in its March 7, 1938, pre-release review:

> Everything that has made *Flash Gordon* popular in cartoon form is here, all the wildly-imaginative pseudo-scientific fantasy, with roaring rocketships, death-dealing rays, interplanetary warfare, fantastic adventures, the touch of magic. Yet it has all been done with a sincerity which provides an essence of reality.... The result is fascinating.

Three:
Flash Gordon Conquers the Universe (1940)

PRODUCTION CREDITS:

Flash Gordon Conquers the Universe (Universal) Released April 9, 1940 *Producer:* Henry MacRae, *Directors:* Ford Beebe, Ray Taylor, *Screenplay:* George H. Plympton, Basil Dickey, Barry Shipman, *Photography:* Jerry Ash, A.S.C., William A. Sickner, A.S.C., *Supervising Film Editor:* Saul A. Goodkind, *Film Editors:* Joseph Gluck, Louis Sackin, Alvin Todd, *Art Direction:* Harold H. MacArthur, *Dialogue Director:* Jacques Jaccard, *Assistant Directors:* Edward Tyler, Charles Gould. *Sound System:* Western Electric. Running Time: 235 minutes.

CAST:

Buster Crabbe *(Flash Gordon)*, Carol Hughes *(Dale Arden)*, Charles Middleton *(Emperor Ming)*, Anne Gwynne *(Sonja)*, Frank Shannon *(Dr. Zarkov)*, John Hamilton *(Prof. Gordon)*, Herbert Rawlinson *(Dr. Frohmann)*, Tom Chatterton *(Prof. Arden)*, Shirley Deane *(Princess Aura)*, Roland Drew *(Prince Barin)*, Lee Powell *(Capt. Roka)*, Donald Curtis *(Ronal)*, Don Rowan *(Captain Torch)*, Victor Zimmerman *(Thong)*, Edgar Edwards *(Turan)*, Ben Taggart *(Gen. Lupi)*, Michael Mark *(Karm)*, Luli Deste *(Queen Fria)*, Earl Dwire *(Jenda)*, Carmen D'Antonio *(Ming's dancing girl)*, Harry Bradley *(Keedish)*, Sigurd Nilssen *(Count Korro)*, Mimi Taylor *(woman)*, Byron Foulger *(Druk)*, William Royle *(Capt. Suden)*, Ernie Adams *(bit part)*, Roy Barcroft *(Ming soldier/adjutant/Arborian sentry)*, Robert Blair *(bit)*, Jean Brooks *(bit)*, Allan Cavin *(Ming's death dust experiment subject, intelligent man)*, Jack Roper *(Ming's death dust experiment subject, man of low intellect)*, Lane Chandler *(Ming soldier/adjutant)*, Chief Yowlatchie *(king of rock people)*, Mala *(prince of rock people)*, Harold Daniels *(bit)*, Paul Douglas *(bit)*, John Elliott *(bit)*, Jack Gardner *(bit)*, Pat Gleason *(bit)*, Reed Howes *(bit)*, Bill Hunter *(bit)*, Eddie Parker *(bit)*, Ernie Payson *(bit)*, Joey Ray *(bit)*, Paul Reed *(bit)*, Charles Sherlock *(bit)*, Clarice Sherry *(bit)*, Charles Waldron, Jr. *(bit)*.

CHAPTER TITLES:

(1) "The Purple Death," (2) "Freezing Torture," (3) "Walking Bombs," (4) "The Destroying Ray," (5) "The Palace of Terror," (6) "Flaming Death," (7) "The Land of the Dead," (8) "The Fiery Abyss," (9) "The Pool of Peril," (10) "The Death Mist," (11) "Stark Treachery," (12) "Doom of the Dictator"

FEATURE VERSIONS:

The Purple Death from Outer Space (1966, 88 minutes), and *Perils from the Planet Mongo* (1966, 91 minutes), both released for television and non-theatrical distribution.

VIDEO AVAILABILITY:

Both the complete serial and the two feature versions have been released on DVD by Image Entertainment.

······················

Chapter 1: "The Purple Death"

Synopsis

A virulent plague known as the purple death — leaving a tell-tale purple spot on the foreheads of its victims — ravages the Earth, and the world's greatest scientists, led by Professor Gordon (Flash Gordon's father), meet to combat the pandemic. Professor Gordon's son Flash, who, in an effort to discover the plague's origins, is exploring the outer reaches of the Earth's atmosphere in a rocketship with Dr. Zarkov and Dale Arden, radios his father when they see a Ming ship from the planet Mongo discharging a strange dust toward the Earth. Flash and Zarkov attack the Ming ship, engaging the craft in battle. They are almost downed by the alien ship's heat ray, but manage to escape by taking evasive action. Flash radios his father that the dust emitted by Ming's rocketship is causing the purple death, and informs him that he, Zarkov and Dale are flying to Mongo so that they can eliminate the plague at its source.

Arriving on the planet Mongo, they are greeted in the forest kingdom of Arboria by their old friend Prince Barin, now happily married to Ming's daughter, Aura. In Barin's palace a banquet is held in honor of Queen Fria, ruler of Frigia, a frozen kingdom to the north. The Earth people are introduced to the haughty Fria, who is also seeking Barin's aid against Ming.

Meanwhile, in his palace, Ming, evil ruler of Mongo, receives a report from Captain Torch, who had piloted the death dust rocketship, that he has destroyed Zarkov's ship. Torch is unaware that Flash Gordon and Zarkov have survived the battle. Ming then confers with his scientist, Jenda, who informs him that he has refined the death dust, perfecting it so that the purple death will kill only people of high intelligence — leaving those of low intellect alive to serve as Ming's slaves. Jenda then invites Ming to a demonstration in the laboratory that evening, and Ming, intrigued, agrees to attend.

In Barin's palace, Queen Fria and Barin receive word that Fria's General Lupi has been captured by Ming. Barin, Flash, Zarkov and Barin's men Roka, Ronal and Count Koro all board Zarkov's rocketship in an effort to rescue the General. Landing in a secluded area near Ming's palace, they gain entry when Captain Suden, one of Barin's agents operating undercover in the palace, opens a door for them by remote control.

Ming, who is attending the scientist Jenda's ruthless experiment in the laboratory, watches callously as an intelligent test subject is killed by Jenda's refined death dust. Ming intends to kill General Lupi in the same manner when a security alarm sounds. Flash and

Charles Middleton returns as Ming the Merciless in *Flash Gordon Conquers the Universe* (1940).

In chapter 1 of *Flash Gordon Conquers the Universe*, Flash and his friends join Prince Barin in an alliance against Ming. From left: Donald Curtis, Frank Shannon, Carol Hughes, Buster Crabbe, Luli Deste, Sigurd Nilsen, Roland Drew, Shirley Deane.

the others are now in the palace laboratory, and Zarkov stays behind to destroy Ming's lab, while Flash interrupts Ming's death dust experiment with a raygun blast.

A fight erupts and the enraged Ming flees. Flash battles Ming's soldiers, and as he struggles with one man of enormous size and strength, Flash is hurled into a deep flaming pit...

Comments

With Charles Rogers ousted as studio head in yet another Universal management crisis, new studio boss Cliff Work restored Henry MacRae to his former position as head of the studio's serial department.

Filmed from November 27, 1939, to December 22, 1939, at a final cost of $177,000 ($8,000 over the estimated budget), *Flash Gordon Conquers the Universe* was the cheapest of the *Flash Gordon* serials, and was completed more quickly than the others, finishing in less than four weeks (despite troubled location shooting in Red Rock Canyon, 130 miles from Los Angeles, due to cloudy weather).

Carol Hughes and Buster Crabbe in a publicity photo for *Flash Gordon Conquers the Universe.*

Studio memos reveal that considerable effort was made by producer Henry MacRae to hold costs down to a bare minimum, with MacRae saving on miniature expenses by reusing several rocketship scenes from the first serial (these were often modified with optical work, such as snow printed onto the original shot when the rocketship is supposedly landing in a frozen area).

Although a more sophisticated optical process was used to represent the various death rays and raygun blasts in a few sequences, in most scenes the effect was achieved by simply *scratching* animated raygun blasts directly onto the film emulsion.

Despite this severe economizing, *Flash Gordon Conquers the Universe* is one of the sound era's best serials, and, with its bright, sharp, glossy photography, certainly one of the prettiest to *look* at. The sleeker visuals were an attempt to emulate the more sophisticated comic strip artwork produced by Alex Raymond at the time. For instance, a stunning glass art shot of Ming's palace throne room is expertly rendered and blended into the real scenery.

The music score for *Universe* employs the same themes used in the first two serials, somewhat re-orchestrated, with the notable addition of Franz Liszt's *Les Preludes*, used to magnificent effect over the credits of each chapter, and also in many scenes.

World War II had officially begun in Europe only a couple of months before shooting began on *Universe*, and the reality of global turmoil seems to have intruded on the serial's fantasy at times. Pointed references abound to *dictator* Ming, and to the prisoners being mistreated in Ming's "filthy concentration camps." In fact, this time out, Ming seems less the mythic representation of evil that he was in the first two serials than a run-of-the-mill tyrant, fighting ruthlessly against those who oppose him politically in order to maintain his illegitimate power base.

Jean Rogers, under contract to 20th Century–Fox at the time and unavailable to Universal for the role of Dale Arden, was replaced by Carol Hughes. A pretty, 29-year-old brunette, Hughes was a more-than-adequate substitute, and displayed plenty of shapely leg in a miniskirt outfit worn in several episodes.

Other casting changes included Roland Drew portraying a leaner, more handsome Prince Barin, and Shirley Deane as Princess Aura. Deane had originally been cast as the title character in Columbia's *Blondie* series but was replaced by Penny Singleton when the on-screen chemistry between Deane and Arthur (Dagwood) Lake didn't gel. Deane is adequate as Princess Aura, but is somewhat colorless. Apparently, in *Universe* Aura's lustful tendencies (so ably displayed by Priscilla Lawson in the first serial) have been curbed by Barin, and she seems thoroughly domesticated by this point — much to the disappointment of male viewers.

....

Chapter 2: "Freezing Torture"

Synopsis

As Flash plunges downward into the pit, he manages to save himself by grabbing the metal rung of a ladder embedded in the rocky wall of the shaft. The man he had been fighting is dead, having fallen into the flaming depths of the pit. Zarkov, having sabotaged

Ming's laboratory with an explosive charge, arrives just in time to lower a cable into the pit and save Flash. Together they leave the palace, unaware that Barin's ally Ronal has been left behind in the pit room.

As Ronal, unseen in an isolated corner, slowly regains his composure, Ming arrives in the pit room with Captain Torch. Infuriated by the near-destruction of his laboratory, Ming, fearful that Dr. Zarkov may discover polarite, a mineral that neutralizes the death dust, demands the immediate capture of Flash Gordon and Zarkov, offering Torch a lavish reward. Ronal overhears this and, stealthily leaving the pit room, rejoins Flash, Zarkov, the rescued General Lupi and the others at the rocketship.

Zarkov's rocketship blasts off, but is spotted by a fleet of Ming's bombers. The bombers engage Zarkov's ship in an air battle, and even though Ming's ships are much faster, Zarkov escapes by activating a device that makes his rocketship invisible. Returning to Barin's palace, Flash, Zarkov and Barin, along with Dale, Roka and Ronal, lay plans for a journey to the icy sub-zero kingdom of Frigia, where polarite can be mined. They are unaware that their plans have been overheard by Sonja, a beautiful young girl who is Ming's spy in Barin's palace.

Flash, Dale, Zarkov, Barin, Roka and Ronal journey to Frigia in Zarkov's rocketship, protected from the extreme low temperatures by heavy clothing and a counter-freeze spray invented by Zarkov. Dale slips as they climb an icy wall but is rescued by Flash, and they finally arrive near a deposit of polarite. A rocketship piloted by Ming's captain Torch, circling overhead, spots the Zarkov expedition below and drops a bomb on a nearby peak, causing a catastrophic avalanche that sweeps toward Flash, Zarkov and the others...

Comments

Chapters 2 and 3 contain stock footage culled from the imported German mountain-climbing docudrama *White Hell of Pitz Palu* (directed by Leni Riefenstahl), which had been released in America by Universal in 1930. The borrowed mountain-climbing and avalanche footage works well editorially, providing some badly-needed physical scope for these scenes, but the grainier visual quality resulting from copying the shots makes their insertion rather obvious. Oddly, a spectacular shot of a group traveling over snowy ridges on skis is used in the opening titles of each chapter, but appears nowhere in the serial itself. The ice scenes showing Buster Crabbe and the other *Universe* actors were filmed on the studio's backlot Nagana Rocks set, re-dressed with snow, ice, and silver paint to simulate the sub-zero environment of Frigia.

We get a hint of the planet Mongo's economic system in chapter 2; the reward offered by Ming for the capture of Flash and Zarkov is 100,000 "Mingos"!

· · · · · · · · · · · · · · · · · · · ·

Chapter 3: "Walking Bombs"

Synopsis

Although the Zarkov expedition has survived the avalanche caused by Ming's bombers, Flash, Dale, Roka and Barin (who has been injured) have been swept into an icy crevice,

Flash (Buster Crabbe) and Dale (Carol Hughes) battle one of Ming's explosive robots.

where they struggle to survive against the bitter cold. They are finally rescued and pulled from the crevice by Zarkov and the others, who have been frantically searching for them.

At Ming's palace Captain Torch reports that Flash Gordon and Dr. Zarkov have been killed by the avalanche, but Ming receives a message from radio operator Tekla confirming that they have survived. Enraged, Ming offers Torch one last chance, ordering Torch and his assistant Thong back to Frigia with a cargo of "annihilatons"—exploding, remote-controlled robots that will be used to attack the Zarkov expedition.

In Frigia, Flash and Dale are supervising the excavation of polarite when the Ming ship piloted by Torch and Thong lands behind a ridge. The annihilatons are unloaded and prepared; Torch activates them by remote control from within the ship and marches the robots around the hill. The annihilatons attack Flash's party, and Ronal, seeing the robots approach, runs to Zarkov's rocketship to inform Zarkov.

Meanwhile, Flash and Dale try to escape the annihilatons by climbing the face of a cliff, but Dale slips and falls to the ground. Flash jumps back down to help Dale and attacks one of the annihilatons just as Torch, in the Ming ship, explodes the robot by remote control...

Top: One of Ming's robots menaces Carol Hughes in *Flash Gordon Conquers the Universe*, chapter 3. *Bottom:* Flash (Buster Crabbe) tries to rescue Dale (Carol Hughes) from Ming's robot.

Comments

The *Just Imagine* idol footage of "the Great God Tao" was revived again for this serial, with shapely dancer Carmen D'Antonio cavorting for Ming's entertainment as though she is a member of the stock footage chorus line. D'Antonio, who appeared in several films, was known for a slightly risqué "Hot Voodoo" nightclub dance act, which is presented in sanitized form here.

The design of Zarkov's rocketship has been upgraded a bit since the first serial, with a more detailed and convincing interior, and a remodeled exit/entrance ladder built into the inside of the ship's door. The miniature rocketships have also been improved; they are more smoothly controlled in flight (sometimes shown at a 3/4 angle to give the shot depth), with superior exhaust action.

The lead characters underwent some modification in *Universe*; Dale Arden is described at one point as "a chemist and a radio operator," elevating her somewhat from her previous "damsel in distress" niche represented by Jean Rogers.

Zarkov is more forceful; whereas Flash Gordon had been firmly in charge of events and decision-making in the first two serials, it is Zarkov who seems to be in control here, sometimes overruling Flash and directing the others in their struggle against Ming.

....

Chapter 4: "The Destroying Ray"

Synopsis

Flash is thrown into a nearby bomb crater when the annihilaton explodes, but survives. Under Torch's control, an annihilaton picks up the unconscious Dale, while Zarkov is also captured and brought to Torch's ship.

Barin finds Flash, stunned but alive. In his ship, Torch tells Dale and Zarkov that Flash is dead and flies back to Ming's palace with them. Ronal, who has also survived the exploding annihilatons, has witnessed Torch's abduction of Dale and Zarkov. He informs Flash of this, but Flash must delay any rescue attempt because of the purple death; the elimination of the plague must take priority, even over the lives of Dale and Zarkov.

Flying back to Earth in the rocketship with Roka, Flash radios his father that he has obtained the polarite and will drop a large quantity of it atop Mt. McKinley, which will attract all of the death dust on Earth and nullify its effects. After this is accomplished, and the threat of the purple death is ended, Flash returns to Mongo to rescue Dale and Zarkov.

In Ming's palace throne room, Dale and Zarkov are brought before a gloating Ming, who threatens Zarkov with torture and demands that Dale be "dressed in garments befitting the wife of an emperor."

Captain Torch has been ordered by Ming to retrieve Zarkov's rocketship from Frigia, but, returning to the frozen kingdom, Torch and Thong are startled to see the ship flying over Frigia as Flash and Roka return from Earth. Aware that they have been spotted by Torch, Flash simulates a fire aboard the rocketship to make it appear as though it has crash-landed in Frigia. When Torch and Thong also land, and when they go to Flash's ship to investigate, Flash ambushes and captures them.

In chapter 4 of *Flash Gordon Conquers the Universe* (1940), Ming (Charles Middleton) forces Dale (Carol Hughes) to watch as Zarkov is executed.

Flash and Roka, with Torch and Thong prisoners, fly the Ming ship back to Ming's palace. Leaving Torch and Thong tied up in the ship, they enter the palace grounds. Torch, screaming for help from inside the ship, alerts passing Ming soldiers, who attack Flash and Roka, but Flash and Roka overpower them in a fight and continue on to Ming's palace.

In the palace, Ming and his retinue watch as Zarkov, condemned to death, is manacled between two pillars as Dale is forced to witness his execution by death ray. Flash and Roka cautiously enter the palace and overhear two Ming soldiers discussing Zarkov's fate. They attack the soldiers, and as Roka continues the fight, Flash moves on, entering Ming's torture chamber just as the death ray erupts from a clock mechanism on the wall and begins to move toward Zarkov. As Flash tries to free Zarkov before the ray can strike, they are both trapped in the searing light beam. Ming roars with maniacal laughter and Dale screams in terror...

Comments

Chapter 4 uses medieval sets from the Rowland V. Lee production *Tower of London* (1939) to good effect. The concluding scene showing Ming's staged execution of Zarkov (as a helpless, screaming Dale is forced to watch) is one of the very best in this serial, capturing the adventurous, romantic essence of Alex Raymond's characters.

....

Chapter 5: "The Palace of Terror"

Synopsis

As Flash and Zarkov writhe in pain when Ming's death ray strikes them, Roka, having overpowered Ming's soldiers, suddenly appears and destroys the death ray mechanism with a raygun blast. Dale stops a soldier who tries to fire on Roka, and Flash and Roka manage to escape the torture chamber, although they are forced to leave Zarkov behind. Dale is taken away and confined with another girl prisoner, and Ming offers Zarkov his life if he will use his genius in Ming's service. Taken to Ming's laboratory, Zarkov meets Karn, a fellow scientist who is also being held prisoner, and conspires with him against Ming.

Flash and Roka discover an entrance to the underground caverns beneath the palace. After fighting more of Ming's soldiers, the duo take their uniforms as a disguise and re-enter the palace in search of Dale, whom they locate and free. Flash and Roka take Dale to Zarkov, but Zarkov decides to stay in the laboratory with Karn so that, working together, they can sabotage Ming's plans for conquest. Zarkov pre-sets twin portable radios at a specific wavelength so that he and Flash can maintain contact. They are surprised by a

Dale (Carol Hughes, second from left) is rescued by Flash (Buster Crabbe).

Ming soldier, who orders the other soldier (actually Roka in disguise) to arrest Flash, while Ming is notified. When the soldier leaves, Flash, Roka and Dale escape, and when Ming learns of this he orders them recaptured.

After secretly communicating with Flash by radio, Zarkov leaves the lab in disguise to meet Flash, leaving Karn behind. Torch, aware that Flash, Dale and Zarkov have escaped and will attempt to take off in a rocketship, sabotages the ship with explosives. Roka, who is ambushed by a Ming soldier when he approaches the ship to wait for Flash, Dale and Zarkov, is thrown into the booby-trapped ship during the fight, and the ship, bursting into flame, accidentally takes off with Roka inside. Flash, Dale and Zarkov arrive in time to see this and take off in a Ming ship to save Roka. Swinging onto the burning rocketship on a cable connected to the other ship, Flash is able to save both Roka and himself just before the Ming ship explodes.

Two of Barin's ships, one commanded by Barin himself, approach. Believing they are the enemy (it is, after all, a Ming ship), Barin prepares to destroy the enemy craft. Frantically trying to communicate with Barin, Flash and Zarkov find that the radio in the Ming ship is disabled. Unaware that his friends are in the Ming ship, Barin fires on them with his destructo ray, blasting them from the sky...

Dale (Carol Hughes) is abducted by Ming. The bit player at right is Jean Brooks, later featured in the Val Lewton films *The Leopard Man* and *The 7th Victim*.

Comments

Actress Jean Brooks (Jeanne Kelly), who would be featured in the classic Val Lewton horror thrillers *The Leopard Man* and *The Seventh Victim* at RKO a few years later, has a bit part in chapter 5.

....

Chapter 6: "Flaming Death"

Synopsis

Unable to communicate with Barin's ship and identify themselves, Flash desperately uses the ray cannon of the Ming ship to send a dot-and-dash code message. Receiving the message and realizing his friends are aboard the Ming ship, Barin orders his men to cease firing and prepares a magnetic grappling mechanism that allows Flash, Dale, Zarkov and Roka to transfer to his ship when they pull alongside.

Zarkov has learned from his ally Karn that Ming has a terrible new weapon, a fire projectile capable of raining mass destruction from the skies, and is told that Ming will

Dale (Carol Hughes) and Flash (Buster Crabbe) test the contrathermal device in *Flash Gordon Conquers the Universe*.

test the weapon on a remote section of Barin's kingdom, Arboria. Fearing for his daughter Aura's safety, Ming sends a message by carrier bird to his agent Sonja, operating undercover in Barin's palace as one of Aura's attendants, ordering her to prepare for Aura's abduction.

Aura is deceived into visiting impoverished woodcutters in Arboria's Red Forest, where Ming's operatives kidnap her. At Ming's palace, a distraught but defiant Aura is taken before her father, who orders her imprisoned.

Meanwhile, Barin's scientist Keedish, working with Zarkov, has invented a contrathermal device that nullifies zultrilnillium, the power behind the fire projectiles. Receiving word that Barin and his friends will attempt to stop the projectiles as they are launched, Ming attempts to disrupt Barin's communications by sending Torch and Sonja to destroy Barin's radio room.

The contrathermal devices are installed in a rocketship, and Flash, along with Dale and Ronal, blasts off to await the arrival of Ming's fire projectiles. Ming launches the first projectile from a huge cannon outside his laboratory. Flash and Dale see the flaming missile from their ship, and as it strikes the ground, exploding into a searing conflagration, they land nearby.

Flash, dressed in a protective fireproof suit, leaves the rocketship with one of the contrathermal devices, which diminishes the flames as he plants it in the ground nearby. Although weakened by the heat, Flash returns to the ship and retrieves another contrathermal unit to repeat the procedure. But as he nears the blistering fires, a connection burns out in the overloaded control unit inside the ship, exposing Flash to the overpowering heat...

Comments

Twenty-two-year-old starlet Anne Gwynne, first glimpsed briefly in chapter 1, returns as the treacherous Sonja in this episode to play a major supporting role for the balance of the serial. A few years later, Gwynne would be featured in the Universal thriller *House of Frankenstein*.

The production team's efforts to reflect the increasingly more polished style of Alex Raymond's comic strip is in full evidence here, with several horses made up to look like unicorns during the Red Forest abduction of Aura.

....

Chapter 7: "The Land of the Dead"

Synopsis

As the contrathermal control unit fails, Flash stumbles into a nearby pit. When the unit restarts, he climbs safely out of the pit and returns to the rocketship. Over Dale's objections, Flash grabs another contrathermal unit and once again exits the ship to combat the flames. Due to Flash's efforts, the fires are extinguished, and Ronal radios Barin's palace with the news. But Barin's radio communications are knocked out by an explosion from an attacking Ming ship (piloted by Torch, Thong and Sonja) before Barin can tell Flash, Dale and Roka where Ming's other fire projectiles have fallen.

Torch's ship is attacked by Barin's defense squadron, but Torch escapes by faking a crash, and radios Ming from Arboria. Ming, furious that his fire projectiles are being nullified, begins to suspect that there is a traitor in the palace.

While Thong stays with their rocketship, Torch and Sonja manage to sneak into Barin's palace. Zarkov has designed a nullitrion gun, capable of paralyzing Ming's power plants, and Barin and Roka make plans to transport the weapon to the giant Dome Rock in the Land of the Dead, where it can be focused on Ming's headquarters. Torch appears in the laboratory and, having overheard their plans, tries to destroy the nullitrion gun, but is driven away when Roka suddenly hurls a flask of exploding chemicals at him.

In Ming's palace, Ming has been informed of Zarkov's nullitrion gun. Ming orders Captain Torch to follow the Zarkov expedition to the Land of the Dead and plant a powerful bomb on Dome Rock, where he knows Zarkov will install the device. As Torch, Thong, Sonja, and Ming's soldiers arrive in the Land of the Dead and proceed to plant the bomb, Sonja, watching from afar, is suddenly ambushed by several Rock Men, a race of primitives wearing costumes textured like rock so that they can blend into the surrounding terrain. When the Rock Men are menaced by a huge reptile, they evade the monster by surrounding the captive Sonja and seemingly fading into the rocky cliff area. Sonja is taken to a nearby cave.

Flash and his friends journey to the Land of the Dead. From left: Frank Shannon, Buster Crabbe, Carol Hughes, Roland Drew.

Flash's expedition arrives in the Land of the Dead. From left: Roland Drew, Lee Powell, Carol Hughes, Buster Crabbe, Frank Shannon.

Flash, Dale, Zarkov, Barin and Roka land in their rocketship nearby. The Rock Men see Torch and Ming's soldiers planting the bomb and capture them. As Flash, Dale, and Zarkov approach the area, the Rock Men attack them, and the bomb planted by Torch and his men, operating on a timing fuse, suddenly explodes...

Comments

Chapter 7 introduces the Rock People, a primitive race speaking an indecipherable language, achieved on the soundtrack by playing normal dialogue *backwards*! Inspiration was apparently beginning to lag by this point; although the Rock People work well enough as characters and as a plot device, they are too reminiscent of the Clay People in *Flash Gordon's Trip to Mars*, even to the point of the filmmakers reusing the Clay People's Franz Waxman *Bride of Frankenstein* music motif.

Chapter 8: "The Fiery Abyss"

Synopsis

The massive explosion shakes the entire area, with Flash, Dale, Barin and Roka knocked unconscious by the blast. The Rock Men carry them to a nearby cliff area where gas is released from the surrounding rocks. They are revived by the vapors, as Torch and his men watch. Zarkov, who understands their strange language, acts as interpreter, and tells Flash that they are accused of causing the explosion from Torch's bomb, and are to be taken before the Rock King, along with Torch and his men.

En route, they are attacked by another giant reptile, and are instructed to remain motionless in the rocks until it passes. But one of Torch's men panics and, running away, is devoured by the monster.

Taken into a huge cave located nearby, they are brought before the Rock King, who, passing judgment, blames them for the disappearance of his son, missing since the explosion. The Rock King sentences them all to death unless his son is returned. When Flash

Flash and his friends are held captive by the Rock People. From left, in center: Lee Powell, Frank Shannon, Buster Crabbe, Carol Hughes and (seated) Chief Yowlatchie.

resists, he is beaten senseless by the Rock Men. Flash eventually regains consciousness in a cave cell, where he has been imprisoned with Zarkov and Roka. Zarkov theorizes that since the Rock Men speak an ancient language similar to that once spoken by long-ago inhabitants of the Gobi desert on Earth, they must be descended from "the original race" that colonized several planets in the solar system.

Dale and Sonja have been confined together in another cell, and Sonja, who is supposedly asleep, secretly watches as Dale attempts to call Karn on the radio. Sonja takes the radio from Dale and calls Karn again, this time while Ming is present in the laboratory. Realizing that Karn is the traitor who has revealed his technological secrets to Zarkov and Flash Gordon, the furious Ming orders Karn arrested, to await execution.

In their cell, Flash and Zarkov formulate an escape plan. Roka pretends to be ill, and when the Rock Man guard enters the cell to investigate, Flash and Zarkov manage to escape. Fleeing the cave, they go to search for the Rock King's son so that they can return him to his father and save the others.

As Roka and Dale are prepared for execution by the Rock People, along with Sonja, Torch and his men, Flash and Zarkov discover the missing Rock Prince pinned to a cliff, held captive by the strong magnetic pull of a giant lodestone uncovered by Torch's explosion. Flash attempts to dislodge the lodestone by rolling a huge boulder at it, and sends Zarkov back to the Rock King to tell him that they have found his lost son.

In the rock cave, though, the Rock People have already executed one of Torch's men by tossing him into a flaming pit. They prepare to do the same to Dale, as Zarkov is delayed by another giant reptile on his way back to the cave...

Comments

The "giant" lizard footage shot for the first serial is revived for these chapters, probably as an economy move. This actually works better than the viewer might expect, particularly in a scene where one of Torch's men is attacked and eaten by one of the beasts. Oddly, the lizard footage is not printed in slow motion (to impart an illusion of great size) as it was in the first serial, but is seen here at normal speed.

....

Chapter 9: "The Pool of Peril"

Synopsis

Zarkov escapes from the giant reptile and is rejoined by Flash, who has managed to knock the lodestone into a deep pit, saving the Rock Prince. Sending Zarkov ahead to tell the Rock King his son is alive, Flash carries the Rock Prince back to the cave. Dale and Roka, who have attempted to escape, have been recaptured by the Rock Men, but are set free by the grateful Rock King when Flash arrives with the king's son.

In the confusion, Torch, Sonja and Thong escape and are pursued across the rough terrain of the Land of the Dead by Flash, Dale, Zarkov and Roka. Torch, Sonja and Thong are surprised by an attacking reptile, and when Sonja screams in terror, Barin, waiting at the rocketship in the distance, hears her and spots Torch, Thong and Sonja with binoculars. He sounds

Roka (Lee Powell), Flash (Buster Crabbe), Dale (Carol Hughes) and Zarkov (Frank Shannon) in the Land of the Dead.

the ship's alarm siren to alert Flash and the others, and as Flash, Dale, Zarkov and Roka rush Torch's party, Torch tries to hold them off by rolling boulders down a rocky incline at them.

Several Rock Men, led by the Rock Prince, arrive and help Flash capture Torch, Sonja and Thong, who has been knocked unconscious in a struggle with Flash. After thanking the Rock People, Flash, Dale, Zarkov, Roka and Barin take Torch, Sonja and Thong aboard their rocketship as prisoners and fly back to Arboria, where Barin hatches a plan to rescue Aura from Ming.

Flash tries to call Karn at a predetermined time, but is unsuccessful; Karn, his plotting against Ming discovered, has been imprisoned with Aura. But Captain Suden, Barin's undercover ally in Ming's palace, lets Aura out of the cell, and she is able to retrieve the radio from the laboratory and bring it to Karn. Karn communicates with Flash and Barin, and Barin tells Captain Suden to open the dungeon gates leading into Ming's palace at a pre-set time.

Barin's rocketship, with Flash, Zarkov, Barin and Roka aboard, lands near Ming's palace. Suden opens the dungeon gates by remote control as arranged, and as Flash's party stealthily enter the caverns beneath the palace, they see Ming soldiers approaching. They ambush the soldiers, but as they fight, a palace alarm sounds, alerting Ming, who orders Captain Suden to release flood waters into the dungeon to drown them all...

Comments

The scenes in the Land of the Dead were filmed in Red Rock Canyon (located about 130 miles from Los Angeles), a popular location used in many low-budget westerns and serials. In some long shots (well-disguised) doubles for the actors were used, probably to speed up the location filming; and some rear-projection process shots were also filmed in the studio using the Red Rock location footage.

When the floodwaters are released into the dungeon at the end of this chapter, footage of waterlogged, collapsing mine timbers from the 1927 Universal silent *Perch of the Devil*, used once before in chapter 4 of the first serial, is seen again here.

····················

Chapter 10: "The Death Mist"

Synopsis

Watching on a televisor, Ming sees Flash, Zarkov and the others swept away by the inrushing waters and, believing them dead, leaves the control room to tell Princess Aura.

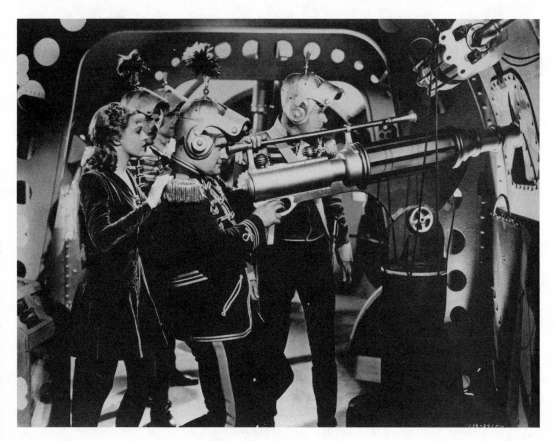

Sonja (Anne Gwynne, left) and Captain Torch (Don Rowan, center) attack Flash's expedition.

Dale is kidnapped by Torch and Sonja in chapter 10 of *Flash Gordon Conquers the Universe*. From left: Buster Crabbe, Lee Powell, Anne Gwynne, Carol Hughes, Don Rowan.

As soon as Ming is gone, Captain Suden opens a side door in the dungeon corridor by remote control, and the water carries Flash and his friends to safety. They return to their rocketship and, with Torch, Sonja and Thong still prisoners, blast off, laying alternate plans for entering the palace.

In Ming's throne room, Aura and Karn are brought before the emperor, and Karn dies a martyr's death when he attacks Ming and is killed by a guard in front of the horrified Aura. Ming has appropriated Karn's radio, and when a call from Zarkov is received, one of Ming's guards imitates Karn's voice in an attempt to lure Zarkov's party into a trap.

In Arboria, Flash and Dale attempt to interrogate Torch and Sonja in their cells, but are unsuccessful. Sonja tries to negotiate with Flash, openly flirting with him, but is rebuffed. Left alone, Torch and Sonja communicate with each other by tapping on their cell walls in code. Sonja fakes her own suicide by hanging to attract Barin's guard; when the guard opens the cell door, she kills him with his own ray gun, then frees Torch.

Flash meets with Zarkov and the others to discuss a radio message received from "Karn." They realize that it was from an imposter, and that Ming knows they are still alive and will attack them.

Flash tells the radio operator that an attack is imminent. After Flash leaves, Torch and Sonja arrive and take control of the radio room, knocking the operator unconscious.

Torch uses the radio to communicate with Ming and learns that Ming is sending a fleet of gas bombers to attack Barin's palace. To insure their success, Torch uses the radio to recall Barin's rocketship patrols.

Meanwhile, Dale and Roka have discovered the dead guard in Sonja's cell and realize their prisoners have escaped. Dale goes to the radio room and is taken prisoner by Torch and Sonja. Flash, informed of Torch and Sonja's escape, arrives too late and is forced back by Torch, who uses Dale as a hostage. Torch locks Flash in the radio room as Ming's gas bombers attack, and retreats to the tower roof with Dale and Sonja. As Flash escapes from the radio room and hurries to the tower roof with Roka, Roka is stunned when Torch fires at him with a raygun, while Dale struggles with Sonja. As Flash and Torch desperately fight each other on the roof, the tower is shaken by one of the gas explosions, and they are both thrown off the roof, hurtling toward the ground below...

Comments

Sets reused from other movies in this chapter included those constructed for the 1940 James Whale production *Green Hell*, with the *Universe* company actually filming on the sets *before* Whale's production team used them.

....

Chapter 11: "Stark Treachery"

Synopsis

Flash and Torch plunge from the tower roof, but are saved when they fall into a moat surrounding the tower. Zarkov, Barin and Roka go to the lab and open the gas control valves, clearing the mist out of the area. Ming's soldiers have landed in a rocketship, though, and have kidnapped Dale and Ronal. Taking Sonja with them, the soldiers revive Dale and Ronal aboard the Ming ship. Barin's patrolling rocketships fire on them, but the Ming ship escapes and returns to Ming's palace.

With Torch held prisoner by Flash and Barin, Sonja, reporting to Ming, suggests that he exchange Dale and Ronal for Torch. Ming calls Flash and Barin at Barin's palace, and they reach an agreement.

Flash and Barin, with Torch as their hostage, meet Ming's soldiers at the determined location and make the exchange. Dale immediately collapses, though, and Zarkov realizes that she has been drugged by Ming. A note from Ming is given to Zarkov by Ronal, and Zarkov learns that he must bring Dale to Ming's palace alone, where she will be given an antidote — otherwise, she will die. Zarkov, helpless, can only do as he has been instructed, and takes Dale to Ming's palace in a rocketship.

Dale's antidote is administered by Ming, but now he holds both Dale and Zarkov prisoner. Flash, Barin and Roka land near Ming's palace in a rocketship, entering the palace through an abandoned subterranean tunnel. In the palace laboratory, Zarkov conspires against Ming with one of Ming's scientists, Druk, while Dale is taken to Aura's locked quarters, which Ming has booby-trapped with an electrified carpet lying on the floor just within the doorway.

Top: Princess Aura is held captive by Ming. From left: Charles Middleton, Don Rowan, Anne Gwynne, Shirley Deane, unidentified. *Bottom:* Flash and Barin attempt to rescue Aura — and encounter one of Ming's former victims! From left: Lee Powell, Roland Drew, Buster Crabbe.

After gaining entry into the palace, Flash arrives at Aura's quarters. With Barin and Roka waiting in the outside corridor, Flash stealthily enters, stepping on the electrified carpet as thousands of volts course through his body...

Comments

The undersea breathing helmets originally worn by the sharkmen in chapter 3 of the first serial — and reused again as gas masks in *Flash Gordon's Trip to Mars* — turn up yet *again* in this chapter, as breathing apparatus used during Ming's gas bomber attack.

....

Chapter 12: "Doom of the Dictator"

Synopsis

Dale, awakened from sleep by Flash's entry into the room, manages to blurt out a warning just as Flash's drawn sword makes contact with the electrified carpet, drawing off most of the charge and saving Flash's life. Flash is only momentarily stunned, and Barin locates a hidden switch on the outer frame of the doorway, turning off the current.

Flash and his friends overpower Ming's forces. From left: Roland Drew, Byron Foulger, Frank Shannon, Buster Crabbe, Shirley Deane, Carol Hughes, Lee Powell.

Flash (Buster Crabbe) bails out of a rocketship just before it crashes into Ming's palace.

Flash, Barin, and Roka take Dale and Aura from the room, but are stopped by Ming's soldiers. Roka, however, who is disguised in one of their uniforms, orders them away. After encountering and battling more of Ming's soldiers, Flash's party gains entrance to the laboratory and are reunited with Zarkov. Ming now knows that Flash, Barin, Dale, Zarkov and Roka are in the laboratory, but they are safely barricaded inside where his soldiers cannot reach them. As Zarkov lays plans to destroy Ming, Ming calls them on the televisor. A defiant Zarkov tells him that he is now in control of the laboratory, the source of all Ming's power, but Ming enigmatically responds that he has another source of power that Zarkov is unaware of. Flash and Roka leave the laboratory through a secret passage, and Flash, spying on Ming, learns that Ming has a "Z-O" ship loaded with powerful solarite, ready to attack the Earth. Flash also learns that Ming intends to double-cross the Earth people and Barin, whether they agree to his terms or not.

With Zarkov clearing Ming's spaceport defenses, Flash steals the Z-O ship and flies it directly toward Ming's palace tower, where the desperate tyrant has confined himself, along with his retinue (including Torch and Sonja). When Ming hears that Dale, Zarkov and the others have left the laboratory, he knows that he is doomed. As Flash's friends blast off in Zarkov's rocketship, Flash bails out of the Z-O ship just before it crashes into the palace tower, killing Ming, Torch, Sonja and everyone else inside.

As he parachutes to safety, Flash is picked up in mid-air by Zarkov's ship. Their mission completed and the Earth once again saved from Ming's evil schemes, Flash, Dale and Zarkov plan their voyage home.

Comments

And so the outer space film exploits of Flash Gordon ended with this episode. At one point in chapter 12, a supporting character remarks that there is a possible escape route for Ming, who is trapped in the palace tower, but that Ming "will be too terrified to think of it," paving the way for a possible sequel that was never to be. Perhaps this was just as well, for after 40 weekly episodes among three serials, encompassing more than 13 hours of total screen time, the material was showing signs of strain; and the serial format itself would lose its appeal with the general public by the end of World War II.

Ming was finally overthrown in Alex Raymond's comic strip as well, after years of epic struggle. Flash Gordon had been the rallying point for the planet Mongo's epic struggle with oppression and Ming's lust for power. The mad monarch's quest for total domination and control of his expanding empire, not to mention his obsession with Dale Arden, had placed him in direct conflict with Flash. But when Ming left the plot, a significant portion of Flash's motivation left with him. An eventual return to Earth and confrontations with the Axis powers of World War II seemed a bit mundane by comparison.

Alex Raymond may have felt the same way, leaving the strip and joining the United States Marine Corps. King Features assigned replacement Austin Briggs to illustrate writer Don Moore's scripts, but soon brought in Emanuel "Mac" Raboy to handle the art. Raboy was an accomplished comic-book artist who brought a beautiful sense of reality to the most fantastic plots and stories. It's a tribute to the strip's unique appeal, as well as the artist's talent, that Raboy would produce Flash Gordon, uninterrupted, for the next 19 years. That's more than 975 pages of consistent, high-quality material, and only his death in 1967 ended his run on the feature.

As for Alex Raymond, he died in an auto accident in 1956. As Buster Crabbe, who met Raymond (the artist told Crabbe that he considered the actor to be "Flash personified"), told author Roy Kinnard, "His [Raymond's] ambition was to own an expensive Italian sports car, and what happened when the poor guy finally got one? He took it out on the road and ended up wrapping himself around a tree." [*Interview*]. It was a tragic end for a titan of pop culture, but his legacy lives on; and to this day, when comic art fans or professional illustrators speak about past masters of the form, Raymond's name is always one of the first mentioned.

Appendix I:
Buck Rogers (1939)

Buck Rogers (Universal) Released April 11, 1939

CREDITS

Producer: Barney Sarecky, *Directors:* Ford Beebe, Saul A. Goodkind, *Screenplay:* Norman S. Hall, Ray Trampe, *Photography:* Jerome Ash, A.S.C., *Art Director:* Ralph M. DeLacey, *Film Editors:* Joseph Gluck, Louis Sackin, Alvin Todd, *Music Director:* Charles Previn, *Sound:* Bernard B. Brown, *Sound System:* Western Electric. Running Time: 237 minutes.

CHAPTER TITLES

(1) "Tomorrow's World," (2) "Tragedy on Saturn," (3) "The Enemy's Stronghold," (4) "The Sky Patrol," (5) "The Phantom Plane," (6) "The Unknown Command," (7) "The Primitive Urge," (8) "Revolt of the Zuggs," (9) "Bodies Without Minds," (10) "Broken Barriers," (11) "A Prince in Bondage," (12) "War of the Planets"

CAST

Larry "Buster" Crabbe *(Buck Rogers)*, Constance Moore *(Wilma Deering)*, Jackie Moran *(George "Buddy" Wade)*, Anthony Warde *(Killer Kane)*, Jack Mulhall *(Capt. Rankin)*, C. Montague Shaw *(Dr. Huer)*, William Gould *(Air Marshall Kragg)*, Philson Ahn *(Prince Tallen)*, Henry Brandon *(Capt. Lasca)*, Wheeler Oakman *(Lt. Patten)*, Kenneth Duncan *(Lt. Lacy)*, Carleton Young *(Scott)*, Reed Howes *(Capt. Roberts)*, Wade Boteler *(Prof. Wade)*, Al Bridge *(dynamo room guard)*, Roy Butler *(control officer)*, Stanley Price *(Capt. Martin)*, Eddy Chandler *(dirigible captain)*, Frank Ellis *(Kane soldier)*, Jack Gardner *(Prof. Huer's lab assistant)*, Lane Chandler *(army official at Wade's lab)*, Kenneth Harlin *(reporter at Wade's lab)*, Karl Hackett *(Councilor Krenko)*, John Harmon *(Hidden City air controller)*, Theodore Lorch *(council member)*, Eddie Parker *(council-room guard)*, David Sharpe *(Kane pilot/Hidden City sentry/Saturnian Lt.)*, Tom Steele *(Kane pilot/Hidden City technician/balcony guard)*.

FEATURE VERSIONS

Planet Outlaws (1953), released theatrically (running time 71 minutes); and *Destination Saturn* (1966), released for television and non-theatrical distribution (running time 91 minutes).

VIDEO AVAILABILITY
The complete serial, *Buck Rogers*, has been released on DVD by VCI.

Synopsis

Chapter 1: "Tomorrow's World"

A huge dirigible piloted by Buck Rogers and his young assistant Buddy Wade is trapped in a polar ice storm and crashes on a frozen mountain peak in the Arctic. A container of experimental "nervano gas" leaks during the crash and preserves Buck and Buddy in a state of suspended animation. Discovered and revived 500 years later by soldiers of the future, they learn that the entire world has been conquered by a super-scientific gangster named Killer Kane and his gang of ruthless cohorts. Transported by their rescuers to the Hidden City, concealed by huge mechanized stone gates opening into a remote mountain, they meet the brilliant Dr. Huer and his pretty assistant Wilma Deering. Learning that Dr. Huer, Wilma and the other Hidden City inhabitants are dedicated rebels opposed to Killer Kane's tyranny, Buck and Buddy agree to help them in their war against Kane. Professor Huer has invented interplanetary spaceships, de-gravity belts, invisibility rays, disintegrator guns, and many other strange and wondrous gadgets in defense of Hidden City and its rebels, but more help is needed. Buck, Buddy and Wilma fly to the planet Saturn to enlist Saturnian aid in their struggle. Just as they reach the distant planet, though, they are bombed by one of Killer Kane's pursuing spaceships.

Chapter 2: "Tragedy on Saturn"

Buck, Buddy and Wilma save themselves by escaping to the surface of Saturn with their de-gravity belts. Killer Kane's men, led by the ruthless Captain Lasca, follow them. After a desperate fight, Buck and his friends are overpowered by their attackers. Both groups are then captured by Saturnians and taken before the Council of the Wise for questioning. The devious Lasca convinces the council members that Killer Kane is a benevolent ruler and that Buck and his friends are troublesome revolutionaries. Buck, Wilma and Buddy, seeing that they are about to be jailed, break free and return to Earth using one of Lasca's spaceships. As they attempt to pilot the craft through the huge stone gates of the Hidden City, Buck and his friends are nearly killed when the massive gates suddenly close and crush the ship.

Chapter 3: "The Enemy's Stronghold"

Buck, Wilma and Buddy escape with their de-gravity belts after Buck uses a raygun to blast a hole in the floor of the spaceship. A Saturnian prince, Tallen, arrives on Earth to sign a peace treaty with Killer Kane. Buck and Buddy, learning of this, invade Kane's heavily-guarded palace in an attempt to prevent such an alliance. Confronting Kane, Buck convinces Tallen that Kane is a despot, and, using their de-gravity belts, Buck and Buddy

Wilma (Constance Moore), Buck (Buster Crabbe) and Buddy (Jackie Moran) are captured by Killer Kane's forces in chapter 2 of *Buck Rogers* (1939).

exit through a nearby window with Tallen. They float safely to ground level, but Kane's guards open fire on them with a paralyzer ray.

Chapter 4: "The Sky Patrol"

Buddy manages to destroy the paralyzer ray machine with his disintegrator gun, saving Buck and Tallen. Stealing one of Kane's spaceships, they fly back to Hidden City, but Wilma, spotting the Kane spaceship and unaware that Buck and Buddy are in the ship with Tallen, bombs it, forcing the craft down into the mountainous terrain below. As Buck, Buddy and Tallen try to reach safety, they are trapped in an explosion caused by a pursuing Killer Kane ship.

Chapter 5: "The Phantom Plane"

Realizing that Buck, Buddy and Tallen are being attacked by Kane's men, Wilma abruptly changes course and drives Kane's forces away with her spaceship. She then picks

Buck Rogers (1939), chapter 4: Buck (Buster Crabbe), Tallen (Philson Ahn) and Buddy (Jackie Moran) escape Kane's troops.

up her friends, and they return to Hidden City, where Tallen signs the agreement officially pledging Saturn's aid in the rebels' war against Kane. Unable to communicate this news to Saturn due to radio interference, Buck, Wilma, and Tallen journey to Saturn in a spaceship to consolidate the treaty. Discovering an empty Killer Kane ship when they arrive on Saturn, they board it and try to wreck the controls. Captain Lasca and his men, hidden nearby, ambush them and inject gas into the ship, knocking out Buck, Wilma, and Tallen.

Chapter 6: "The Unknown Command"

Buck and his friends are removed from the gas-filled ship by Lasca's men and taken before the Saturnian Council of the Wise. Lasca's men outfit Tallen with a mind-controlling filament concealed inside his helmet. A puzzled Buck and Wilma hear Tallen denounce them before the council and order their imprisonment, unaware that Tallen's will is under Lasca's domination. Grabbing Lasca's raygun and using Tallen as a shield, Buck and Wilma escape in a subterranean tunnel car. Attempting to prevent their escape, Lasca throws a lever closing the huge steel tunnel doors, and the speeding car crashes into the barrier.

Chapter 7: "The Primitive Urge"

Buck and his friends survive the crash, and Buck (finally realizing how Tallen has lost his will) removes the mind-controlling filament from Tallen's helmet. His mind now restored, Tallen recognizes Buck and Wilma as his friends, and they return to the Council of the Wise, where the misunderstanding is rectified. Lasca has discovered that an outcast race of hideous Saturnian primitives, the Zuggs, worship a robotized victim of Lasca's as a god, and that the Zuggs are planning a revolt. Using the human robot to lead a Zugg mob, Lasca and his men take control of the uprising. The enraged Zuggs charge Buck, who is overwhelmed by the savage mob.

Chapter 8: "Revolt of the Zuggs"

Escaping through a secret door, Buck rallies the Saturnian guards, overpowering Lasca and his human robot as they are inciting the Zuggs to further violence. Removing the mind-controlling filament from the robot's helmet, Buck restores the man (a former Killer Kane soldier) to normalcy. In gratitude, he tells the Zuggs, who still worship and obey him, to lay down their arms. Grateful to Buck for his suppression of the Zugg revolt, the Saturnian Council of the Wise agrees to consolidate Saturn's alliance with the Hidden City rebels against Killer Kane. Returning to Earth, Buck's spaceship is attacked by Kane's forces and plunges from the sky when it collides head-on with an enemy ship.

Chapter 9: "Bodies Without Minds"

Buck manages to regain control of his ship and make a safe landing, but he and Wilma are captured by Kane's men and taken to Kane's palace, where Wilma is imprisoned

Buck argues his case before the Saturnian Council of the Wise. Front four, from left: Henry Brandon, Philson Ahn, Buster Crabbe, Constance Moore.

and Buck is outfitted with a mind-control helmet. Dr. Huer and the rulers of Hidden City believe that Buck and Wilma have been killed, but Buddy Wade, confident they are still alive, risks his life to invade Kane's stronghold and rescue them. Finding Kane's council room empty, Buddy activates the tele-eye viewing device and sees Buck in Kane's dynamo room, where Buck, wearing a mind-control helmet, has been transformed into a human robot. Just as Buddy leaves the council room to help Buck, he is shot by one of Killer Kane's guards and falls out of a window.

Chapter 10: "Broken Barriers"

Buddy, only stunned by the shot, manages to find Wilma. Freeing Buck from the mind-control helmet, they escape in one of Kane's spaceships and return to Hidden City, unaware that a Kane spy is hiding in the ship. Once inside Hidden City, the spy calls Kane's headquarters, revealing the location of the rebel stronghold. As Kane's bombers fly toward Hidden City, Buck discovers the Kane spy and, in a tense struggle, is shot by a ray-gun.

Chapter 11: "A Prince in Bondage"

As Kane's squadron bombs Hidden City, Buck, only slightly injured by the raygun blast, overpowers the Kane spy and hurriedly closes the city gates, barring entry to all but the first of Kane's bombers. Buck and Buddy travel to Saturn to rally Saturnian aid in the battle, only to find that Tallen is being held captive by Lasca, who has demanded that the Saturnians capitulate to Kane's domination. Buck urges the Saturnian rulers to refuse. As Kane's bombers arrive and bomb Saturn, Buck and Buddy try to escape in the underground tunnel car. But when a Kane bomb explosion causes the tunnel roof to collapse, Buck is pinned beneath the falling debris.

Chapter 12: "War of the Planets"

Buck frees himself from the rubble with his disintegrator gun, and Buck, Buddy and Tallen capture Lasca and his soldiers. With the Saturnians pledging their help in the war against Kane, Buck and Buddy return to Earth. In a massive air battle, Kane's forces are defeated. As a reward for his selfless and courageous efforts, Buck is promoted in rank by his Hidden City superiors, and, with the peace of the world secure, his thoughts turn to romance with Wilma.

Buck (Buster Crabbe) pilots a spaceship in *Buck Rogers* (chapter 11).

Comments

Buck Rogers is generally regarded as the first true science fiction newspaper strip. The basic concept originally appeared in a novel, *Armageddon 2419 A.D.*, published in a 1928 issue of *Amazing Stories* magazine. This was the story of Anthony Rogers, who is trapped in a mine and overcome by a mysterious gas. When he awakens, five hundred years in the future, he finds Earth overrun by a global civil war, and soon joins the forces battling evil Mongolian hordes.

This story caught the attention of John F. Dille, head of the National Newspaper

925-68-EP12

Killer Kane (Anthony Warde, coat being gripped by Buster Crabbe) is defeated in the final chapter of *Buck Rogers* (1939). Jackie Moran is second from left.

Syndicate. He asked the story's writer, Philip Nowlan, to adapt his tale as the basis of a daily newspaper comic strip. Drawn by artist Dick Calkins, the strip, now called *Buck Rogers*, debuted on January 7, 1929. The strip was an immediate hit, and a color Sunday page was added on March 30, 1930. Despite Calkins' uneven artwork (or perhaps because of its appealing crudeness), the public enthusiastically responded to the imaginative exploits of Buck, his sidekick Wilma Deering, her brother Buddy, and Dr. Huer. A true pop-culture phenomenon, the strip was published continuously until it ended in 1967.

Seeking a follow-up to their popular *Flash Gordon* serials, Universal Pictures negotiated a deal with the John F. Dille Syndicate for the production of two *Buck Rogers* serials, only one of which was eventually made. The resulting film, one of the best sound movie serials ever made, shares the same art director, basic visual design, music and star (Buster Crabbe) with the previous year's *Flash Gordon's Trip to Mars*, and could be considered an unofficial "fourth" *Flash Gordon* serial — hence its inclusion as an appendix here.

Buck Rogers was shot from September 6 to October 21, 1938, at a final cost of $185,000 — $3,000 *more* than *Flash Gordon's Trip to Mars*. The production went over budget; it had been estimated at $177,000 and approved at $177,200.

After beginning with miniature work, the actors began shooting on location in Red Rock Canyon on Monday, September 19, 1938, returning to the studio on Thursday, September 22. All scenes with the actors were completed by October 14, and the remaining miniature photography was wrapped on October 21.

By October 28, 1938, the serial was in the hands of Universal's editors, and the music score was recorded on December 9.

A December 20, 1938, memo from Universal Studios manager M. F. Murray to studio executive Maurice Pivar and *Buck Rogers* co-director Saul A. Goodkind verifies that the release prints of *Buck Rogers* utilized the same Kodak Sonochrome Verdante color film stock used for *Flash Gordon's Trip to Mars*. So, like *Flash Gordon's Trip to Mars*, *Buck Rogers* was tinted green on its original release.

Even though many props and set designs from the two previous *Flash Gordon* serials reappear here, art director Ralph DeLacy made a commendable effort to avoid further similarities to the *Flash Gordon* serials whenever possible, designing boxy, angular spaceships that look nothing like the rocketships in the *Flash Gordon*s. More (previously unused) stock footage from Fox's *Just Imagine* turns up, with the vast futuristic cityscapes from the earlier film representing villain Killer Kane's *Buck Rogers* super-city. Like *Flash Gordon's Trip to Mars*, *Buck Rogers* features a music score that is mostly recycled *Bride of Frankenstein* motifs, but re-orchestrated for this serial. The explanatory recap titles at the head of every chapter slant backwards and scroll off into infinity in a style that was copied by George Lucas for the opening titles in *Star Wars* (1977).

As Buck Rogers, Buster Crabbe (with his natural dark hair) turns in his usual competent performance. His casting draws inevitable comparisons between *Buck Rogers* and *Flash Gordon*; in fact, Mexican posters are in existence suggesting that, south of the border at least, *Buck Rogers* was re-titled and marketed as a *Flash Gordon* serial.

As Wilma Deering, 18-year-old Constance Moore is a perfect choice — pretty but not overly glamorous, and believable in her role. Jackie Moran (who had a small role in *Gone with the Wind* the same year), as Buddy Wade, plays the sort of extraneous but popular juvenile sidekick character common in serials and comic books of the period; and C. Montague Shaw (the king of the Clay People in *Flash Gordon's Trip to Mars*) is properly benign and authoritative as Dr. Huer.

Buck Rogers, released as a 12-chapter serial, was originally planned as a 13-chapter production. An extra episode, consisting mainly of recap footage from previous chapters, was prepared, and was originally intended to be chapter 7. According to the late film historian George Turner, the storyline of this 22-minute chapter, of which bootleg 16mm prints have circulated, is as follows:

> Dr. Huer and Air Marshall Kragg receive a radio report from Buck Rogers on the planet Saturn informing them that an alliance with the rulers of Saturn has been confirmed. Dr. Huer and Kragg then discuss what a godsend Buck Rogers has been to the Hidden City rebels' struggle against Kane. Using flashbacks, the narrative then repeats Buck's first appearance before the Saturnian Council of the Wise, when Captain Lasca turns the Council against Buck and Wilma. Then Lasca and Tallen are shown visiting Killer Kane on Earth, and Buck exposes Kane's tyranny to Tallen. Buck, Buddy and Tallen escape. Buddy is injured in the escape, and Tallen is captured by Lasca and robotized, betraying Buck. Tallen is kidnapped by Lasca, and Lasca uses another robotized victim to control the Zuggs. The chapter ends with the Zuggs overthrowing their Saturnian masters.

Except for the framing dialogue between Dr. Huer and Kragg, lasting only a couple of minutes, the entire chapter was cobbled together from previously-seen footage, and was

Dr. Huer demonstrates a new weapon in chapter 4 of *Buck Rogers*. From left: C. Montague Shaw, Philson Ahn, unidentified, Buster Crabbe, Constance Moore.

probably dropped by Universal because it was such an obvious cheat (as it is, the final 12-chapter release version has flashbacks in chapters 9 and 11). Nevertheless, the extra chapter (designated 7-B) was made available to theaters wishing to exhibit it and expand the serial's running time by an extra week.

Universal prepared a 7-reel re-edited feature version of *Buck Rogers* for theatrical release entitled *Planet Outlaws*. This feature was later acquired, along with the *Buck Rogers* serial, the *Flash Gordon* serials, and several other Universal serials (along with their feature versions) by New York theater owner and independent producer-distributor Sherman S. Krellberg. Krellberg re-released these films profitably in the late 1940s and early 50s under his Goodwill and Filmcraft distribution banners. In 1953, Krellberg altered *Planet Outlaws* somewhat from its original form, adding new footage (which doesn't make very much sense) of a narrator discussing the possibility of interplanetary invasions. The credits for Krellberg's revised version of *Planet Outlaws* list Harry Revier (who had directed Krellberg's 1935 serial *The Lost City*) as director, with the new dialogue written by Helen Leighton and Revier, and the new footage intercut by editors Renault Revier and Joseph Sorbera.

Planet Outlaws is rarely seen today. A second, completely different *Buck Rogers* feature version, running 91 minutes and titled *Destination Saturn*, was re-edited from the serial for TV distribution in 1966. *Destination Saturn* has been misleadingly distributed on video as *Planet Outlaws*, and picked up another bogus title in the early 1980s when it was distributed on cassette by Magnetic Video as *Buck Rogers Conquers the Universe*.

In the late 1960s, the original serial version of *Buck Rogers*, along with the three *Flash Gordon* serials, were released to television by A.B.C. Films, Inc. The serial was the complete 12-chapter release version, though the re-made main title cards read *Buck Rogers vs. the Planet Outlaws*. When the rights to the serial were later acquired by Crystal Pictures, *Buck Rogers* received limited play at revival theaters after the release of *Star Wars*. It was again distributed to TV, and again the prints were complete (although of somewhat lesser quality), this time bearing Filmcraft's theatrical re-release main titles. It is this print that currently appears on DVD from VCI Entertainment.

There was a very low-budget TV series, *Buck Rogers in the 25th Century*, broadcast live on ABC from 1950 to 1951, starring Robert Pastene as Buck and Lou Prentis as Wilma Deering. A 1979–81 NBC TV series, starring Gil Gerard as Buck and Erin Gray as Wilma, also spawned a 1979 theatrical feature. The original Buck Rogers himself, Buster Crabbe, guest starred on a highly-rated episode of the NBC series.

Appendix II: Filmographies

This section contains select filmographies for fifty of the most prominent actors, producers, directors, writers and technicians involved in making the Flash Gordon *serials, and is intended to provide an overview of their careers. Entries are listed alphabetically by the subject's last name.*

Richard Alexander (November 19, 1902–August 9, 1989)

Actor, "Prince Barin" in *Flash Gordon* and *Flash Gordon's Trip to Mars*. Onscreen from 1926. Adaptable to either villainous or heroic roles, and one of classic Hollywood's most dependable character actors, Richard Alexander brought conviction and believability to every role he played. Alexander may not have been the most *convincing* of actors (he has noticeable difficulty with some of the flowery dialogue in *Flash Gordon*), but he had a dramatic presence that cannot be denied, and a sincerity that led directors like Cecil B. DeMille to use him regularly. Alexander was only 33 years old in *Flash Gordon*; prematurely balding, he looked much older. His facial characteristics, along with his burly, imposing physique, made him just as forceful in more sinister parts; a good example would be his role as the dastardly El Lobo in the 1937 Republic serial *Zorro Rides Again*. 1926: *Old Ironsides*; 1927: *The King of Kings*; 1928: *The Mysterious Lady*; *The Cameraman*; *The Viking*; 1930: *All Quiet on the Western Front*; 1931: *The Front Page*; *Dirigible*; 1932: *Skyscraper Souls*; *The Sign of the Cross*; 1933: *Queen Christina*; 1934: *The Scarlet Empress*; *Cleopatra*; 1934: *Babes in Toyland*; 1935: *Annie Oakley*; *The Miracle Rider* (serial); *The Crusades*; *The Fighting Marines* (serial); 1936: *The Story of Louis Pasteur*, *Flash Gordon* (serial); *The Clutching Hand* (serial); *The Plainsman*; *Follow the Fleet*; *Modern Times*; 1937: *S.O.S. Coast Guard* (serial); *Zorro Rides Again* (serial); 1938: *Flash Gordon's Trip to Mars* (serial); *Flaming Frontiers* (serial); *Marie Antoinette*; *Charlie Chan in Honolulu*; 1939: *Union Pacific*; *Captain Fury*; *Tower of London*; 1940: *Strange Cargo*; *The Great Dictator*; 1941: *The Iron Claw* (serial); 1942: *The Ghost of Frankenstein*; *Reap the Wild Wind*; 1945: *The House of Fear*; 1947: *Unconquered*; 1948: *Joan of Arc*; 1949: *The Fighting Kentuckian*; 1953: *The Band Wagon*; 1954: *The Long, Long Trailer*; 1965: *Requiem for a Heavyweight*; *The Great Race*; 1966: *A Big Hand for the Little Lady*.

Jerome Ash (January 8, 1892–January 5, 1953)

Cinematographer, co-photographed *Flash Gordon, Flash Gordon's Trip to Mars* and *Flash Gordon Conquers the Universe*. Active from 1921. 1925: *The Phantom of the Opera* (visual effects photography); 1930: *The King of Jazz*; *The Cat Creeps*; 1931: *Graft*; 1936: *Flash Gordon* (serial); 1937: *Jungle Jim* (serial); 1938: *Red Barry* (serial); *Flash Gordon's Trip to Mars* (serial); 1939: *The Phantom Creeps* (serial); *Buck Rogers* (serial); 1940: *The Green Hornet* (serial); *Flash Gordon Conquers the Universe* (serial); 1941: *The Green Hornet Strikes Again* (serial); *Buck Privates*; *Never Give a Sucker an*

Richard Alexander (helmeted), as Prince Barin, flies his newfound friends to King Vultan's sky city in an effort to rescue Dale and Thun in *Flash Gordon*, chapter 5. From left, Frank Shannon, Priscilla Lawson, and Buster Crabbe.

Even Break (2nd unit photography); 1942: *The Mad Doctor of Market Street*; 1944: *Abbott & Costello in Society*; 1945: *Pillow of Death*; 1946: *The Time of Their Lives* (visual effects photography); 1948: *Abbott & Costello Meet Frankenstein* (visual effects photography).

Earl Askam (1895–April 3, 1940)

Actor, "Officer Torch" in *Flash Gordon*. Onscreen from 1930. 1930: *Madame Satan*; 1934: *Our Daily Bread*; 1936: *The Great Ziegfeld*; *Flash Gordon* (serial); *Cain and Mabel*; *The Plainsman*; 1937: *You Only Live Once*; *Dead End*; 1939: *Union Pacific*; *Daredevils of the Red Circle* (serial); *Golden Boy*; 1940: *Dark Command*; *Northwest Mounted Police*.

Ford Beebe (November 26, 1888–November 26, 1978)

Director, co-directed *Flash Gordon's Trip to Mars* and *Flash Gordon Conquers the Universe*. Began as a screenwriter; active from 1916.

Ford Beebe was once described as being a director who was "an expert at making something out of nothing"—in other words, a hack. While there may be an element of truth in this back-handed compliment, as even a cursory perusal of his selected credits here will indicate, Beebe's skill

Earl Askam, as Officer Torch (left), is ordered to execute Flash (Buster Crabbe, center) in chapter 10 of *Flash Gordon*. Also pictured are Frank Shannon, Richard Alexander, and Jean Rogers.

in assembling low-budget studio potboilers on schedule and on budget is impressive. It takes something more than a hack to complete a five-hour epic serial like *Flash Gordon's Trip to Mars* in five weeks for a mere $182,000. Even a director as noteworthy as Alfred Hitchcock was impressed by the speed and economy of Beebe's B-mystery *Night Monster* (1942), and complimented Beebe on his achievement. 1930: *The Indians Are Coming* (serial; wrote); 1931: *The Vanishing Legion* (serial); 1932: *The Shadow of the Eagle* (serial); *The Last of the Mohicans* (serial); 1935: *The Adventures of Rex and Rinty* (serial); 1936: *Ace Drummond* (serial); 1937: *Jungle Jim* (serial); *Secret Agent X-9* (serial); *Tim Tyler's Luck* (serial); *Wild West Days* (serial); *Radio Patrol* (serial); 1938: *Flash Gordon's Trip to Mars* (serial); *Red Barry* (serial); 1939: *The Phantom Creeps* (serial); *Buck Rogers* (serial); 1940: *The Green Hornet* (serial); *Flash Gordon Conquers the Universe* (serial); *Junior G-Men* (serial); *Fantasia* (segment); 1941: *The Green Hornet Strikes Again* (serial); *Sky Raiders* (serial); *Sea Raiders* (serial); 1942: *Night Monster*; *Don Winslow of the Navy* (serial); 1943: *Adventures of Smilin' Jack* (serial); *Son of Dracula* (produced only); 1944: *The Invisible Man's Revenge* (directed and produced); 1949: *Bomba, the Jungle Boy* (and sequels).

Carroll Borland (February 25, 1914–February 3, 1994)

Actress, one of Ming's women in *Flash Gordon*. Onscreen from 1933. A groundbreaking and influential distaff bloodsucker in M-G-M's 1935 horror thriller *Mark of the Vampire*, Carroll Borland was only 22 years old in *Flash Gordon*. She could well have been cast in a larger role (she could easily have played Princess Aura) but was instead relegated to a minor supporting part. Well-versed in the works of Shakespeare, Borland had the physical appeal *and* intellectual qualities of a first-rate actress; but she did not fare well in Hollywood, and her considerable potential went unrealized.

1933: *Me and My Pal* (short); 1935: *Mark of the Vampire*; *China Seas*; 1936: *Flash Gordon* (serial); 1983: *Scalps*; 1985: *Biohazard*.

Buster Crabbe (February 17, 1907–April 23, 1983)

Actor, "Flash Gordon" in *Flash Gordon, Flash Gordon's Trip to Mars* and *Flash Gordon Conquers the Universe*. Onscreen from 1930. The king of the serials, Buster Crabbe's film career mirrored that of his rival Johnny Weissmuller in many ways; both began as superlative athletes who then entered the film industry and enjoyed initial public enthusiasm before their careers arced and declined into B-movie tedium. Crabbe did fare a little better than Weissmuller; long-time *Tarzan* and *Jungle Jim* star Weissmuller never escaped the backlot jungles, whereas Crabbe, who was a better actor and more adept with dialogue, enjoyed a wider variety of roles. By 1943, only three years after his final outing as Flash Gordon, Crabbe's Paramount contract had been cancelled and his stock in Hollywood had declined considerably. But he continued on, starring in cheap PRC westerns popular with rural audiences, and his name still had value with the juvenile Saturday matinee serial crowd. Producers like Sam Katzman exploited Crabbe's appeal on into the 1950s. Crabbe's abilities as an athlete gave him the leverage to enter the movies, and his screen notoriety enabled him to enjoy a later career as a successful businessman. He was even, at one point, the "star" of his own comic book, and although he was never accorded the respect he deserved by Hollywood, he served as a positive role model for generations of American youth.

1930: *Good News*; 1932: *The Most Dangerous Game*; 1933: *Island of Lost Souls*; *King of the Jungle*; *Tarzan the Fearless* (serial); 1934: *You're Telling Me*; 1936: *Drift Fence*; *Desert Gold*; *The Arizona Raiders*; *Flash Gordon* (serial); 1938: *Flash Gordon's Trip to Mars* (serial); *Red Barry* (serial); 1939: *Buck Rogers* (serial); *Million Dollar Legs*; 1940: *Flash Gordon Conquers the Universe*; 1941: *Billy the Kid Wanted* (and sequels); 1943: *Devil Riders*; 1944: *Nabonga*; *The Contender*; 1945: *His Brother's Ghost*; 1946: *Swamp Fire*; 1947: *The Sea Hound* (serial); 1950: *Captive Girl*; *Pirates of the High Seas* (serial); *King of the Congo* (serial); 1960: *Gunfighters of Abilene*; 1965: *The Bounty Killer*; *Arizona Raiders*; 1980: *Alien Dead*; 1982: *The Comeback Trail*. TV series: *Captain Gallant of the Foreign Legion* (1955–57).

Donald Curtis (February 27, 1915–May 22, 1997)

Actor, "Captain Ronal" in *Flash Gordon Conquers the Universe*. Onscreen from 1940.

1940: *Flash Gordon Conquers the*

Buster Crabbe as Flash.

Universe (serial); *Northwest Mounted Police*; *Tear Gas Squad*; *Junior G-Men* (serial); *Knute Rockne, All-American*; 1942: *Invisible Agent*; 1943: *Swing Shift Maisie*; *The Cross of Lorraine*; 1944: *National Velvet*; 1945: *Spellbound*; *They Were Expendable*; 1948: *The Fuller Brush Man*; 1955: *It Came from Beneath the Sea*; 1956: *Earth vs. the Flying Saucers*; *The Ten Commandments*; 1967: *Warning Shot*. TV series: *Detective's Wife* (1950).

Herbert Dalmus

Writer, co-wrote *Flash Gordon's Trip to Mars*. Active from 1938.

1938: *Flash Gordon's Trip to Mars*; 1941: *Pals of the Pecos*; *Saddlemates*; *Sailors on Leave*; 1942: *North of the Rockies*; 1944: *Address Unknown*; *An American Romance*; 1947: *Last of the Redmen*; 1948: *Adventures of Don Juan*; 1954: *Star of India*.

Carmen D'Antonio (November 29, 1911–February 9, 1986)

Dancer-actress, Ming's Dancing girl in *Flash Gordon Conquers the Universe*. Onscreen from 1939.

1939: *Another Thin Man*; *Destry Rides Again*; 1940: *Flash Gordon Conquers the Universe* (serial); *Road to Singapore*; 1942: *Arabian Nights*; 1944: *Cobra Woman*; *The Mask of Dimitrios*; *Kismet*; 1947: *Jack Armstrong* (serial); 1951: *Sirocco*; 1953: *Salome*; *The Sins of Jezebel*; 1959: *Tank Commandos*.

Carmen D'Antonio and Charles Middleton in a publicity pose for *Flash Gordon Conquers the Universe* (1940).

Shirley Deane (March 16, 1913–April 26, 1983)

Actress, "Princess Aura" in *Flash Gordon Conquers the Universe*. Onscreen from 1935.

1935: *Dante's Inferno*; 1936: *King of Burlesque*; *Charlie Chan at the Circus*; *Girls' Dormitory*; *One in a Million*; 1937: *On the Avenue*; *Off to the Races*; *Nancy Steele Is Missing*; 1938: *Love on a Budget*; *Prairie Moon*; 1940: *Flash Gordon Conquers the Universe* (serial); *Private Affairs*; 1957: *Kill Me Tomorrow*.

Luli Deste (November 7, 1901–July 7, 1951)

Actress-author, "Queen Fria" in *Flash Gordon Conquers the Universe*. Onscreen from 1932.

1932: *My Friend the King*; 1937: *Thunder in the City*; *She Married an Artist*; 1940: *Flash Gordon Conquers the Universe* (serial); *Ski Patrol*; *South to Karanga*; 1941: *The Case of the Black Parrot*; *Outlaws of the Desert*.

Basil Dickey (November 23, 1880–June 17, 1958)

Writer, co-wrote *Flash Gordon* and *Flash Gordon Conquers the Universe*. Active from 1916.

1933: *Tarzan the Fearless* (serial); *Gordon of Ghost City* (serial); 1934: *The Perils of Pauline* (serial); *The Vanishing Shadow* (serial); *Tailspin Tommy* (serial); 1935: *Tailspin Tommy in the Great Air Mystery*

Shirley Deane (center) as Princess Aura in *Flash Gordon Conquers the Universe* (1940). With Carol Hughes and Charles Middleton.

(serial); *The New Adventures of Tarzan* (serial); 1936: *Flash Gordon* (serial); 1938: *The Spider's Web* (serial); 1939: *The Phantom Creeps* (serial); *Mandrake the Magician* (serial); *Scouts to the Rescue* (serial); 1940: *The Green Hornet* (serial); *Flash Gordon Conquers the Universe* (serial); 1941: *The Green Hornet Strikes Again* (serial); *Holt of the Secret Service* (serial); 1942: *Captain Midnight* (serial); 1944: *Captain America* (serial); *The Tiger Woman* (serial); *Haunted Harbor* (serial); 1945: *The Purple Monster Strikes* (serial); 1946: *The Crimson Ghost* (serial); 1947: *The Black Widow* (serial); 1949: *Federal Agents vs. Underworld, Inc.* (serial).

Roland Drew (August 4, 1900–March 17, 1988)

Actor, "Prince Barin" in *Flash Gordon Conquers the Universe*. Onscreen from 1926.

1937: *Some Blondes Are Dangerous*; 1938: *The Adventures of Tom Sawyer*; *The Goldwyn Follies*; *The Lady in the Morgue*; *The Last Warning*; 1939: *Mystery of the White Room*; *Hitler–Beast of Berlin*; *The Invisible Killer*; 1940: *Flash Gordon Conquers the Universe* (serial); *The Saint Takes Over*; *Wildcat Bus*; 1941: *Sergeant York*; 1942: *The Man Who Came to Dinner*; *All Through the Night*; *Captains of the Clouds*; *Murder in the Big House*; *Across the Pacific*; 1943: *Princess O'Rourke*; *The Desert Song*; 1944: *The Adventures of Mark Twain*; *The Contender*.

Richard Fryer (1894–February 9, 1953)

Cinematographer, co-photographed *Flash Gordon*. Active since 1914.

1914: *America*; 1931: *Strictly Dishonorable* (2nd unit); 1934: *The Perils of Pauline* (serial); *Pirate Treasure* (serial); *The Vanishing Shadow* (serial); *Tailspin Tommy* (serial); 1935: *Tailspin Tommy in the Great Air Mystery* (serial); *The Adventures of Frank Merriwell* (serial); *Stormy*; 1936: *Flash Gordon* (serial); *Ace Drummond* (serial); 1937: *Secret Agent X-9* (serial); 1944: *A Voice in the Wind*.

Wyndham Gittens (February 7, 1885–June 18, 1967)

Writer, co-wrote *Flash Gordon's Trip to Mars*. Active from 1917.

1929: *The Fatal Warning*; *The King of the Kongo*; 1931: *The Vanishing Legion* (serial); 1932: *The Shadow of the Eagle* (serial); *The Last of the Mohicans* (serial); *The Hurricane Express* (serial); 1933: *The Three Musketeers* (serial); *The Whispering Shadow* (serial); *The Mystery Squadron* (serial); 1936: *Ace Drummond* (serial); 1937: *Secret Agent X-9* (serial); *Radio Patrol* (serial); *Tim Tyler's Luck* (serial); 1938: *Flash Gordon's Trip to Mars* (serial); 1939: *Scouts to the Rescue* (serial); 1941: *Holt of the Secret Service* (serial); 1942: *Captain Midnight* (serial).

Muriel Goodspeed (1918–?)

Actress, "Zona" in *Flash Gordon*. Onscreen from 1936.

1936: *Flash Gordon* (serial); 1940: *Bitter Sweet*; 1942: *I Married an Angel*; 1943: *Presenting Lily Mars* (voice only).

Anne Gwynne (December 10, 1918–March 31, 2003)

Actress, "Sonja" in *Flash Gordon Conquers the Universe*. Onscreen from 1939.

This likable Universal starlet (only 22 in *Flash Gordon Conquers the Universe*) was a pretty and competent actress who was a welcome addition to many B-movies and serials of the era. Gwynne's role in *Universe* was a little beyond her range; despite her bitchy, evil sneers, she just seems too wholesomely blonde (and too appealing) to be totally convincing as Sonja.

1939: *Charlie McCarthy, Detective*; 1940: *The Green Hornet* (serial); *Black Friday*; *Flash Gordon*

Sonja (Anne Gwynne, right) and Dale (Carol Hughes) are sentenced to death by the Rock People in chapter 8 of *Flash Gordon Conquers the Universe* (1940).

Conquers the Universe (serial); 1941: *The Black Cat*; 1942: *Ride 'Em Cowboy*; *The Strange Case of Dr. Rx*; 1944: *Weird Woman*; *Murder in the Blue Room*; *House of Frankenstein*; 1947: *Dick Tracy Meets Gruesome*; 1949: *Arson, Inc.*; 1958: *Teenage Monster*.

Norman S. Hall (July 21, 1896–December 12, 1964)

Writer, co-wrote *Flash Gordon's Trip to Mars*. Active from 1933.

1933: *The Three Musketeers* (serial); *The Whispering Shadow* (serial); 1936: *Ace Drummond* (serial); 1937: *Secret Agent X-9* (serial); *Radio Patrol* (serial); *Tim Tyler's Luck* (serial); 1938: *Flash Gordon's Trip to Mars* (serial); *Red Barry* (serial); 1939: *Buck Rogers* (serial); 1940: *Drums of Fu Manchu* (serial); *The Mysterious Doctor Satan* (serial); 1941: *The Adventures of Captain Marvel* (serial); *Jungle Girl* (serial); *Dick Tracy vs. Crime, Inc.* (serial); 1942: *Spy Smasher* (serial); *Perils of Nyoka* (serial); 1944: *The Topeka Terror*; *The Sheriff of Las Vegas*; 1959: *The Young Land*.

John Hamilton (January 16, 1886–October 15, 1958)

Actor, "Professor Gordon" in *Flash Gordon Conquers the Universe*. Onscreen from 1930.

One of classic Hollywood's best and most professional actors, Hamilton attained pop culture immortality as newspaper editor Perry White in *The Adventures of Superman* TV series.

1937: *The Man Who Cried Wolf*; *One Hundred Men and a Girl*; *Night Club Scandal*; 1938: *Mr. Moto's Gamble*; *Boys' Town*; *Too Hot to Handle*; *Mr. Wong, Detective*; *Angels with Dirty Faces*; 1939: *Devil's Island*; *Three Smart Girls Grow Up*; *Confessions of a Nazi Spy*; *Rose of Washington Square*; *The Angels Wash Their Faces*; *Smashing the Money Ring*; *The Roaring Twenties*; 1940: *Dr. Erlich's Magic Bullet*; *Flash Gordon Conquers the Universe* (serial); *Johnny Apollo*; *Tear Gas Squad*; *They Drive by Night*; *Boom Town*; 1941: *Meet John Doe*; *The Maltese Falcon*; *They Died with Their Boots On*; 1942: *Yankee Doodle Dandy*; *Across the Pacific*; 1943: *Crazy House*; 1944: *Government Girl*; *Captain America* (serial); *Action in Arabia*; *Wilson*; *Maisie Goes to Reno*; 1945: *The Great Flamarion*; *The Naughty Nineties*; *Incendiary Blonde*; *Voice of the Whistler*; 1946: *Blondie's Lucky Day*; *Shadows Over Chinatown*; *The Brute Man*; *The Secret of the Whistler*; 1947: *The Beginning of the End*; *It Happened on 5th Avenue*; *The Secret Life of Walter Mitty*; *Blondie in the Dough*; 1948: *The Babe Ruth Story*; 1949: *The James Brothers of Missouri*; 1950: *Annie Get Your Gun*; *The Flying Missile*; 1958: *Outcasts of the City*. TV series: *The Adventures of Superman* (1953–58).

Robert F. Hill (April 14, 1886–March 18, 1966)

Director-actor-writer, co-directed *Flash Gordon's Trip to Mars*. Active from 1915.

1920: *The Flaming Disc* (serial); 1921: *The Adventures of Tarzan* (serial); 1927: *The Cat and the Canary* (writer); 1929: *The Last Warning* (writer); 1933: *Tarzan the Fearless* (serial); 1937: *Blake of Scotland Yard* (serial); 1938: *Flash Gordon's Trip to Mars* (serial); 1940: *The East Side Kids* (actor); 1943: *After Midnight with Boston Blackie* (actor); *Ghosts on the Loose* (actor).

Carol Hughes (January 17, 1910–August 8, 1995)

Actress, "Dale Arden" in *Flash Gordon Conquers the Universe*. Onscreen from 1935.

Cute and charming, Carol Hughes was an ideal replacement for Jean Rogers as Dale Arden. In *Universe*, Hughes looked considerably younger than her 29 years (a decade older than Jean Rogers had been in *Flash Gordon*), and was still a pretty and glamorous addition to films like *D.O.A.* and *Scaramouche* in the early 1950s.

1936: *The Singing Kid*; *Earthworm Tractors*; *Polo Joe*; 1937: *Renfrew of the Royal Mounted*; 1940: *Flash Gordon Conquers the Universe* (serial); *Flight Angels*; 1941: *Scattergood Baines*; *A Girl, a Guy, and a Gob*; *Emergency Landing*; *Desperate Cargo*; 1942: *I Married an Angel*; *Lucky Jordan*; 1945: *The Naughty Nineties*; 1946: *Joe Palooka, Champ*; *Blondie Knows Best*; 1947: *The Bachelor and the Bobby-Soxer*; 1950: *D.O.A.*; 1952: *Scaramouche*.

Carol Hughes and Buster Crabbe.

Donald Kerr (August 5, 1891– January 25, 1977)

Actor, "'Happy' Hapgood" in *Flash Gordon's Trip to Mars*. Onscreen from 1933.

A former Broadway success who never made the big-time in Hollywood, Kerr worked steadily in the film industry nevertheless, often appearing as a reporter, bellboy or cabdriver. "Happy Hapgood" in *Flash Gordon's Trip to Mars* and "One-Shot Mc-Guire" in the 1940 Bela Lugosi horror opus *The Devil*

Bat (newspaper reporter characters that are virtually interchangeable) are his two most prominent and fondly-remembered roles.

1933: *The Picture Snatcher*; *Bombshell*; 1934: *Palooka*; *Kentucky Kernels*; 1935: *George White's 1935 Scandals*; *The Nitwits*; *Annie Oakley*; *Magnificent Obsession*; 1936: *Swing Time*; *Rose Bowl*; 1937: *Dick Tracy* (serial); *Swing High, Swing Low*; *Kid Gallahad*; *The Big Shot*; *Thoroughbreds Don't Cry*; 1938: *Flash Gordon's Trip to Mars* (serial); *Test Pilot*; *Sinners in Paradise*; *Four Daughters*; *Carefree*; *Room Service*; *Crime Takes a Holiday*; *The Mad Miss Manton*; *Angels with Dirty Faces*; 1940: *The Great Man Votes*; *They Made Me a Criminal*; *Mr. Wong in Chinatown*; *Mr. Smith Goes to Washington*; *The Roaring Twenties*; 1940: *Mexican Spitfire*; *The Fatal Hour*; *The Saint's Double Trouble*; *The Fighting 69th*; *Stranger on the Third Floor*; *Wildcat Bus*; *The Ape*; *The Devil Bat*; *Kitty Foyle*; 1941: *Penny Serenade*; 1942: *The Pride of the Yankees*; *Cat People*; *The Great Gildersleeve*; 1943: *Whistling in Brooklyn*; 1944: *Government Girl*; *The Contender*; *The Mark of the Whistler*; *Murder, My Sweet*; 1945: *The Picture of Dorian Gray*; *Captain Eddie*; *The Naughty Nineties*; 1946: *The Face of Marble*; *Little Giant*; *The Kid from Brooklyn*; *Notorious*; *The Best Years of Our Lives*; 1947: *Buck Privates Come Home*; *Song of the Thin Man*; *Merton of the Movies*; 1948: *Ladies of the Chorus*; *He Walked by Night*; 1949: *Knock on Any Door*; *Manhandled*; *Mighty Joe Young*; *Undertow*; 1950: *Montana*; *The Set-Up*; 1951: *Abbott & Costello Meet the Invisible Man*; *Detective Story*; 1952: *Bonzo Goes to College*; *The Sniper*; *She's Working Her Way Through College*; *Lost in Alaska*; 1953: *Abbott & Costello Meet Dr. Jekyll & Mr. Hyde*; *The Big Heat*; *Calamity Jane*; 1954: *Abbott & Costello Meet the Keystone Cops*; 1955: *Abbott & Costello Meet the Mummy*; *The Desperate Hours*; *Oklahoma!*; 1956: *Friendly Persuasion*; 1964: *Dear Heart*.

Eddie Keyes

Prop man and mechanical effects technician, worked on *Flash Gordon, Flash Gordon's Trip to Mars* and *Flash Gordon Conquers the Universe*. Active since 1924.

1931: *Frankenstein*; 1936: *Flash Gordon* (serial); 1938: *Flash Gordon's Trip to Mars* (serial); 1940: *Flash Gordon Conquers the Universe* (serial); 1939: *Buck Rogers* (serial); 1951: *Abbott & Costello Meet the Invisible Man*; 1953: *Abbott & Costello Meet Dr. Jekyll & Mr. Hyde*; 1957: *The Incredible Shrinking Man*; 1959: *The Monster of Piedras Blancas*; 1964: *Invitation to a Gunfighter*. TV series: 1980: *Magnum, P.I.*; 1982: *Knight Rider*; 1984: *Airwolf*.

Priscilla Lawson (March 8, 1914–August 27, 1958)

Actress, "Princess Aura" in *Flash Gordon*. Onscreen from 1935. Lovely and talented, Priscilla Lawson, a former beauty contest winner and model, had all the qualities necessary for success in Hollywood. She never quite made the big-time, however, for a variety of

Priscilla Lawson as Princess Aura, in a posed shot taken during the filming of *Flash Gordon* (1936), chapter 2.

Buster Crabbe and Priscilla Lawson.

reasons; her professional difficulties, coupled with personal problems (including the loss of a leg during World War II military service), contributed to her premature retirement and early death at the age of 44. Whatever personal setbacks may have befallen her, though, she will always be remembered for her role in *Flash Gordon* by anyone who has seen the film. It's no exaggeration to say that, as Princess Aura, she displays a talent, and makes an emotional connection with the viewer, that is remarkable for a 21-year-old actress interpreting what is essentially a "comic book" role. She was married to actor Alan Curtis.

1935: *The Great Impersonation*; 1936: *Sutter's Gold*; *Flash Gordon* (serial); *The Phantom Rider* (serial); *Rose Bowl*; *College Holiday*; 1937: *King of Gamblers*; *The Last Gangster*; 1938: *Arsene Lupin Returns*; *The Girl of the Golden West*; *Test Pilot*; *Three Comrades*; 1939: *The Women*; 1941: *Billy the Kid*.

John Lipson (January 17, 1901–November 28, 1947)

Actor, "King Vultan" in *Flash Gordon*. Onscreen from 1927.

1934: *Manhattan Melodrama*; *Punch Drunks* (short); *Tailspin Tommy* (serial); *Three Little Pigskins* (short); *The Live Ghost* (short); *Babes in Toyland*; 1935: *The Case of the Curious Bride*; *A Night at the Opera*; *Three Little Beers* (short); 1936: *Flash Gordon* (serial); 1937: *Dizzy Doctors* (short); 1940: *Pardon My Berth Marks* (short); *Boobs in the Woods* (short); 1941: *I'll Never Heil Again* (short); *Never Give a Sucker an Even Break*; *Hellzapoppin'*; 1942: *I Married an Angel*; 1943: *A Blitz on the Fritz* (short); *I Dood It*; 1944: *Kismet*; 1945: *The Clock*; 1946: *Suspense*; 1948: *Three Dancing Daughters*; *Luxury Liner*.

John Lipson as King Vultan (far left) in *Flash Gordon* (1936). With Buster Crabbe, Jean Rogers, Frank Shannon, and Richard Alexander.

Theodore Lorch (September 29, 1973–November 12, 1947)

Actor, Ming's "High Priest" in *Flash Gordon* (episodes 8–13). Onscreen from 1920.

1920: *The Last of the Mohicans*; 1924: *The Sea Hawk*; 1927: *The King of Kings*; 1929: *Show Boat*; 1930: *Whoopee!*; 1931: *The Galloping Ghost* (serial); *The Lightning Warrior* (serial); 1932: *Arsene Lupin*; 1933: *Gabriel Over the White House*; *The Sphinx*; 1934: *Blue Steel*; *The Affairs of Cellini*; *Kid Millions*; 1935: *The Mysterious Mr. Wong*; *Uncivil Warriors* (short); *Mad Love*; *Barbary Coast*; *Annie Oakley*; 1936: *Flash Gordon* (serial); *Show Boat*; 1937: *Dick Tracy* (serial); *Goofs and Saddles* (short); *Madame X*; 1938: *The Fighting Devil Dogs* (serial); 1939: *Buck Rogers* (serial); *Stagecoach*; *We Want Our*

Theodore Lorch (right) as Ming's "High Priest" in *Flash Gordon* (chapter 13). With him is Charles Middleton as Ming.

Mummy (short); *Zorro's Fighting Legion* (serial); 1943: *Spook Louder* (short); *This Land Is Mine*; 1944: *Voodoo Man*; 1945: *If a Body Meets a Body* (short); *Micro-Phonies* (short); 1947: *Half-Wits Holiday* (short); *Body and Soul*; 1948: *Hot Scots* (short).

Henry MacRae (August 29, 1876–October 2, 1944)

Producer (also director and writer), produced *Flash Gordon* and *Flash Gordon Conquers the Universe*. Active from 1913.

1929: *Tarzan the Tiger*; 1930: *The Indians Are Coming* (serial, also directed); 1933: *Gordon of Ghost City* (serial); 1934: *The Perils of Pauline* (serial); *The Vanishing Shadow* (serial); *Tailspin Tommy* (serial); 1935: *Tailspin Tommy in the Great Air Mystery* (serial); *Stormy*; *The Adventures of Frank Merriwell* (serial); 1936: *Flash Gordon* (serial); 1937: *Jungle Jim* (serial); *Secret Agent X-9* (serial); *Tim Tyler's Luck* (serial); 1938: *Red Barry* (serial); 1939: *The Phantom Creeps* (serial); *Scouts to the Rescue* (serial); 1940: *Flash Gordon Conquers the Universe* (serial); *The Green Hornet* (serial); *Junior G-Men* (serial); 1941: *The Green Hornet Strikes Again* (serial); 1942: *Don Winslow of the Navy* (serial); *Junior G-Men of the Air* (serial); 1944: *The Great Alaskan Mystery* (serial); *The Mystery of the Riverboat* (serial).

Charles Middleton (October 3, 1874–April 22, 1949)

Actor, "Ming the Merciless" in *Flash Gordon, Flash Gordon's Trip to Mars* and *Flash Gordon Conquers the Universe*. Onscreen from 1920. As the ultimate villain, the over-the-top, theatrical actor Charles Middleton's bravura hamminess was exactly the style required for serials and horror films. In fact, Middleton's acting is so reminiscent of other heavy-handed performers like Bela Lugosi that it's surprising Middleton did not appear in more horror films of the period. Although he was seen in only one serial prior to *Flash Gordon* (the 1935 Tom Mix cliffhanger *The Miracle Rider*), he would appear in many after his portrayal of Ming the Merciless — besides serving as an excellent foil for Laurel & Hardy. Middleton's other noteworthy roles include the insane, homicidal ranch owner in 1932's *Mystery Ranch*, and the ghost of a wrongly-executed man in the PRC thriller *Strangler of the Swamp* (1946). He even sang and danced a bit in *Duck Soup* (1933) and *Murder at the Vanities* (1934). When the respected actor and Ingmar Bergman collaborator Max Von Sydow played Ming in the 1980 remake of *Flash*

Charles Middleton in a publicity photo for *Flash Gordon's Trip to Mars* (1938).

Gordon, Von Sydow praised Charles Middleton's work in the original serials and freely admitted being influenced by him.

1930: *The Devil's Cabaret* (short); 1931: *The Miracle Woman*; *Caught Plastered*; *Beau Hunks* (short); 1932: *The Hatchet Man*; *The Strange Love of Molly Louvain*; *Mystery Ranch*; *Pack Up Your Troubles*; *The Phantom President*; *I Am a Fugitive from a Chain Gang*; *The Sign of the Cross*; 1933: *Destination Unknown*; *The Bowery*; *Duck Soup*; *Nana*; 1934: *Murder at the Vanities*; *Mrs. Wiggs of the Cabbage Patch*; *Broadway Bill*; 1935: *The Fixer Uppers* (short); *The Miracle Rider* (serial); *Hopalong Cassidy*; 1936: *Flash Gordon* (serial); *Show Boat*; 1937: *The Good Earth*; *Souls at Sea*; *Conquest*; *Stand-In*; 1938: *Jezebel*; *Flash Gordon's Trip to Mars* (serial); *Dick Tracy Returns* (serial); 1939: *Jesse James*; *The Oklahoma Kid*; *Juarez*; *Captain Fury*; *Daredevils of the Red Circle* (serial); *The Flying Duces*; 1940: *The Grapes of Wrath*; *Abe Lincoln in Illinois*; *Flash Gordon Conquers the Universe* (serial); *Virginia City*; *Charlie Chan's Murder Cruise*; *Brigham Young*; *Santa Fe Trail*; 1941: *Western Union*; *Sergeant York*; *Belle Starr*; 1942: *Perils of Nyoka* (serial); 1943: *Spook Louder* (short); *Batman* (serial); *The Black Raven*; *Boobs in the Night* (short); *Crazy House*; 1945: *Kismet*; 1946: *Strangler of the Swamp*; *Spook Busters* (short); *The Killers*; 1947: *Jack Armstrong* (serial); *Unconquered*; *Road to Rio*; 1948: *Mr. Blandings Builds His Dream House*.

Wheeler Oakman (February 21, 1890–March 19, 1949)

Actor, "Tarnak" in *Flash Gordon's Trip to Mars*. Onscreen from 1912.

1928: *Lights of New York*; 1929: *Shanghai Lady*; 1932: *The Airmail Mystery*; 1934: *Palooka*; 1935: *G-Men*; 1936: *Darkest Africa* (serial); *Ghost Patrol*; 1937: *Radio Patrol* (serial); 1938: *Flash Gordon's Trip to Mars* (serial); *Red Barry* (serial); 1939: *Buck Rogers* (serial); 1942: *The Bowery at Midnight*; 1943: *The Adventures of Smilin' Jack* (serial); *The Ape Man*; *Ghosts on the Loose*; 1945: *Brenda Starr, Reporter* (serial); 1946: *Hop Harrigan* (serial); 1947: *Jack Armstrong* (serial); *Brick Bradford* (serial); 1948: *Superman* (serial).

Ella O'Neill

Writer, co-wrote *Flash Gordon*. Active from 1931.

1931: *Heroes of the Flames* (serial); *Battling with Buffalo Bill* (serial); 1933: *Gordon of Ghost City* (serial); 1934: *The Perils of Pauline* (serial); *Pirate Treasure* (serial); *The Vanishing Shadow* (serial); 1934: *Tailspin Tommy* (serial); 1935: *Tailspin Tommy in the Great Air Mystery* (serial); *The Adventures of Frank Merriwell* (serial); 1936: *Flash Gordon* (serial); *The Phantom Rider* (serial); 1938: *Flaming Frontiers* (serial).

James Pierce (August 8, 1900–December 11, 1983)

Actor, "Prince Thun" in *Flash Gordon*. Onscreen from 1924, James Pierce was a former screen Tarzan who married Edgar Rice Burrough's daughter.

1927: *Tarzan and the Golden Lion*; *Wings*; 1932: *Horse Feathers*; *Belle of the Nineties*; 1935: *Goin' to Town*; 1936: *Follow the Fleet*; *The Walking Dead*; *Flash Gordon* (serial); 1937: *You Only Live Once*; 1938: *Charlie Chan in Honolulu*; 1939: *Union Pacific*; *Captain Fury*; *Zorro's Fighting Legion* (serial); 1940: *Strange Cargo*; *Johnny Apollo*; *Northwest Mounted Police*; 1941: *Parachute Battalion*; 1942: *Roxie Hart*; 1946: *Nocturne*; 1947: *My Favorite Brunette*; 1948: *The Miracle of the Bells*; 1950: *The Next Voice You Hear*; *The Killer That Stalked New York*; 1951: *Show Boat*.

George H. Plympton (September 2, 1889–April 11, 1972)

Writer, co-wrote *Flash Gordon* and *Flash Gordon Conquers the Universe*. Active from 1912.

1930: *The Indians Are Coming* (serial); 1933: *Tarzan the Fearless* (serial); *Gordon of Ghost City*

James Pierce, as Prince Thun (far right), along with Flash (Buster Crabbe), Dale (Jean Rogers), and Aura (Priscilla Lawson), escape from Kala's palace only to see a group of flying hawkmen approaching in chapter 5 of *Flash Gordon*.

(serial); 1934: *The Perils of Pauline* (serial); *Tailspin Tommy* (serial); 1935: *Tailspin Tommy in the Great Air Mystery* (serial); *Stormy; The Adventures of Frank Merriwell* (serial); 1936: *Flash Gordon* (serial); 1938: *The Spider's Web* (serial); 1939: *The Phantom Creeps* (serial); *Scouts to the Rescue* (serial); 1940: *The Green Hornet* (serial); *Flash Gordon Conquers the Universe* (serial); *Junior G-Men* (serial); 1941: *The Green Hornet Strikes Again* (serial); *The Spider Returns* (serial); *The Iron Claw* (serial); *Holt of the Secret Service* (serial); 1942: *Captain Midnight* (serial); *Gang Busters* (serial); *Junior G-Men of the Air* (serial); 1943: *The Masked Marvel* (serial); 1945: *Jungle Queen* (serial); *Brenda Starr, Reporter* (serial); 1946: *Son of the Guardsman* (serial); 1947: *The Sea Hound* (serial); *Brick Bradford* (serial); 1948: *Superman* (serial); 1949: *Batman and Robin* (serial); 1950: *Pirates of the High Seas* (serial); *Atom Man vs. Superman* (serial); 1951: *Mysterious Island* (serial); *Captain Video* (serial); 1952: *King of the Kongo* (serial); 1956: *Blazing the Overland Trail* (serial); 1957: *Zombies of Mora Tau*.

Lon Poff (February 8, 1870–August 8, 1952)

Actor, Ming's "High Priest" in *Flash Gordon* (chapters 1–3). Onscreen from 1917.

1923: *Souls for Sale*; 1924: *Dante's Inferno*; *Greed*; 1926: *Mantrap*; 1928: *The Man Who Laughs*; 1928: *Two Tars* (short); 1929: *The Iron Mask*; 1933: *Mystery of the Wax Museum*; *Diplomaniacs*; *Tillie and Gus*; 1934: *Kid Millions*; *The Mighty Barnum*; 1936: *Flash Gordon* (serial); 1937: *You Only Live Once*; 1941: *Sullivan's Travels*; 1942: *I Married an Angel*; 1943: *This Land Is Mine*; 1948: *Joan of Arc*; 1949: *Madame Bovary*; 1951: *Father's Little Dividend*.

Lee Powell (May 15, 1908–July 30, 1944)

Actor; "Captain Roka" in *Flash Gordon Conquers the Universe*. Onscreen from 1936.

1936: *Under Two Flags*; 1937: *The Last Gangster*; 1938: *The Lone Ranger* (serial); *The Fighting Devil Dogs* (serial); 1940: *Flash Gordon Conquers the Universe* (serial); 1942: *Texas Manhunt*; *I Was Framed*; 1942: *Rolling Down the Great Divide*; 1944: *The Adventures of Mark Twain*.

Kane Richmond (December 23, 1906–March 22, 1973)

Actor, one of Queen Azura's "Death Squadron" stratosled pilots in *Flash Gordon's Trip to Mars*. Onscreen from 1929.

1931: *Torchy Passes the Buck*; 1935: *The Lost City* (serial); 1937: *Nancy Steele Is Missing*; 1938: *Flash Gordon's Trip to Mars* (serial); *Boys' Town*; *The Affairs of Annabel*; 1939: *The Return of the Cisco Kid*; *Charlie Chan in Reno*; 1940: *Charlie Chan in Panama*; *Knute Rockne, All-American*; 1942: *Spy Smasher* (serial); 1944: *Roger Touhy, Gangster*; *Haunted Harbor* (serial); 1945: *Brenda Starr, Reporter* (serial); 1946: *The Shadow Returns*; 1947: *Brick Bradford* (serial).

Beatrice Roberts (1905–?)

Actress, "Queen Azura" in *Flash Gordon's Trip to Mars*. Onscreen from 1933. Queen Azura is Beatrice Roberts' most prominent film role. A former beauty contest winner, she makes a strong

Lee Powell (far right) as Captain Roka in *Flash Gordon Conquers the Universe* (1940). From left, Carol Hughes, Roland Drew, Buster Crabbe, and Frank Shannon.

Beatrice Roberts (right), as Queen Azura, with Buster Crabbe and Jean Rogers in a publicity photo for *Flash Gordon's Trip to Mars* (1938).

impression, despite the fact that she is somewhat miscast. As Azura, Roberts is markedly less exotic than the viewer might expect, and seems too "nice"—her overall demeanor seems to be that of a suburban housewife rather than a ruthless interplanetary ruler! In her early thirties at the time, Roberts also introduced a badly needed element of sex appeal to the serial. Soon after her *Trip to Mars* role, Roberts was relegated to supporting parts (she can be glimpsed as a villager in the 1943 Universal film *Frankenstein Meets the Wolf Man*).

1934: *The Return of Chandu* (serial); 1935: *Night Life of the Gods*; *Naughty Marietta*; *China Seas*; 1936: *San Francisco*; 1938: *Flash Gordon's Trip to Mars* (serial); *The Devil's Party*; 1940: *Pioneers of the West*; 1942: *Gang Busters* (serial); *The Mystery of Marie Roget*; *Adventures of the Flying Cadets* (serial); 1943: *Frankenstein Meets the Wolf Man*; *Phantom of the Opera*; 1944: *The Invisible Man's Revenge*; *Dead Man's Eyes*; 1945: *Scarlet Street*; 1946: *The Mysterious Mr. M*; *The Killers*; 1947: *The Egg and I*; 1948: *Mr. Peabody and the Mermaid*; 1949: *Criss Cross*.

Jean Rogers (March 25, 1916–February 21, 1991)

Actress, "Dale Arden" in *Flash Gordon* and *Flash Gordon's Trip to Mars*. Onscreen from 1933. Wide-eyed and heartbreakingly beautiful, Jean was one of the loveliest screen actresses of the 1930s. She was still only 19 years old when *Flash Gordon* completed filming in late February of 1936. She had already appeared in two serials for Universal *(Tailspin Tommy in the Great Air Mystery* and *The Adventures of Frank Merriwell)*, and was seen by producer Henry MacRae as the studio's "serial queen." It was a designation unwanted by Rogers; she longed for roles in feature films, and soon moved on to 20th Century–Fox, where she was cast opposite Glenn Ford in his debut film *Heaven with a Barbed-Wire Fence*. Later signing with M-G-M, she enjoyed a moderately successful career at that studio. She was married to RKO publicist Dan Winkler, by whom she had a daughter. After suffering a series of strokes in her later years, Jean died from complications following surgery in 1991.

1933: *Footlight Parade*; 1934: *Eight Girls in a Boat*; *Dames*; 1935: *Tailspin Tommy in the Great Air Mystery* (serial); *Stormy*; *The Adventures of Frank Merriwell* (serial); 1936: *Flash Gordon* (serial); *My Man Godfrey*; *Ace Drummond* (serial); *Conflict*; *Mysterious Crossing*; 1937: *Secret Agent X-9* (serial); *Night Key*; *Reported Missing*; 1938: *Flash Gordon's Trip to Mars* (serial); *Time Out for Murder*; *While New York Sleeps*; 1939: *Hotel for Women*; *Heaven with a Barbed Wire Fence*; 1940: *The Man Who Wouldn't Talk*; *Charlie Chan in Panama*; *Viva Cisco Kid*; *Brigham Young*; 1941: *Let's Make Music*; *Design for Scandal*; 1942: *Dr. Kildare's Victory*; *Sunday Punch*; *Pacific Rendezvous*; 1943: *Swing Shift Maisie*; *Whistling in Brooklyn*; 1945: *Rough, Tough and Ready*; 1946: *The Strange Mr. Gregory*; 1951: *The Second Woman*.

Jean Rogers, with Buster Crabbe, in a publicity pose for *Flash Gordon* (1936).

Don Rowan (January 22, 1905–February 16, 1966)

Actor, "Captain Torch" in *Flash Gordon Conquers the Universe*. Onscreen from 1932.

1936: *Undersea Kingdom* (serial); *San Francisco*; *The Arizona Raiders*; *The Plainsman*; 1937: *Souls at Sea*; *Charlie Chan on Broadway*; 1939: *The Roaring Twenties*; 1940: *The Green Hornet* (serial); *Flash Gordon Conquers the Universe* (serial); *Johnny Apollo*; *Brother Orchid*; 1941: *Riders of Death Valley* (serial); *Navy Blues*.

Barney A. Sarecky (May 7, 1895–August 10, 1968)

Producer-writer, produced *Flash Gordon's Trip to Mars*. Active from 1930.

1935: *The Miracle Rider* (serial, also wrote); 1936: *Darkest Africa* (serial, also wrote); *Ace Drummond* (serial); 1937: *Radio Patrol* (serial); 1938: *Flash Gordon's Trip to Mars* (serial); *Red Barry* (serial); 1939: *Buck Rogers* (serial); 1942: *Black Dragons*; *The Corpse Vanishes*; *The Bowery at Midnight*; 1943: *The Ape Man*; *Ghosts on the Loose*; 1944: *Voodoo Man*; *Return of the Ape Man*; 1951: *Superman and the Mole Men* TV series: *The Adventures of Superman* (1953–58).

Don Rowan as Captain Torch (holding apparatus), in pursuit of Flash and his friends in *Flash Gordon Conquers the Universe* (chapter 10). From left, Victor Zimmerman, Anne Gwynne, and Roy Barcroft.

Frank Shannon (July 27, 1874–February 1, 1959)

Actor, "Dr. Zarkov" in *Flash Gordon, Flash Gordon's Trip to Mars* and *Flash Gordon Conquers the Universe*. Onscreen from 1912.

1924: *Monsieur Beaucaire*; 1932: *Rasputin and the Empress*; 1935: *G-Men*; 1936: *The Prisoner of Shark Island*; *Flash Gordon* (serial); *Anthony Adverse*; 1937: *The Adventurous Blonde*; 1938: *Flash Gordon's Trip to Mars* (serial); *Torchy Blane in Panama*; *Torchy Gets Her Man*; 1939: *Torchy Blane in Chinatown*; *Union Pacific*; *Torchy Runs for Mayor*; *Torchy Blane, Playing with Dynamite*; 1940: *Emergency Squad*; *Flash Gordon Conquers the Universe* (serial); *The Return of Frank James*; *Wildcat Bus*; *Brigham Young*; 1942: *Reap the Wild Wind*; *The Secret Code* (serial); 1943: *Batman* (serial); *The Phantom* (serial); 1944: *The Desert Hawk* (serial); 1949: *A Dangerous Profession*.

C. Montague Shaw (March 23, 1882–February 6, 1968)

Actor, the "King of the Clay People" in *Flash Gordon's Trip to Mars*. Onscreen from 1926.

1932: *Pack Up Your Troubles*; *The Mask of Fu Manchu*; *The Mummy*; *Rasputin and the Empress*; 1933: *Cavalcade*; *Gabriel Over the White House*; *The Big Brain*; *Dancing Lady*; *Queen Christina*; 1934: *The House of Rothschild*; *The Girl from Missouri*; *Charlie Chan in London*; 1935: *Becky Sharp*; *The*

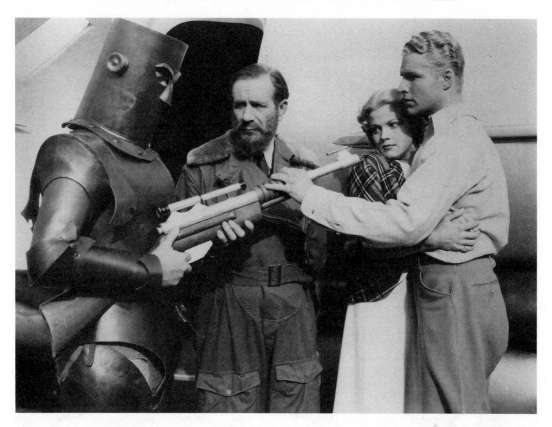

One of Ming's soldiers threatens Zarkov (Frank Shannon), Dale (Jean Rogers) and Flash (Buster Crabbe) with a raygun.

Story of Louis Pasteur; Sylvia Scarlet; a Tale of Two Cities; 1936: *Undersea Kingdom* (serial); *Ace Drummond* (serial); 1937: *Radio Patrol* (serial); 1938: *Flash Gordon's Trip to Mars* (serial); *Suez*; 1939: *Mr. Moto's Last Warning; Buck Rogers* (serial); *Daredevils of the Red Circle* (serial); *Stanley and Livingstone; The Adventures of Sherlock Holmes; The Rains Came; Tower of London; Zorro's Fighting Legion*; 1940: *Charlie Chan's Murder Cruise; The Mysterious Doctor Satan* (serial); 1941: *The Green Hornet Strikes Again* (serial); *Holt of the Secret Service* (serial); *Dick Tracy vs. Crime, Inc.* (serial); 1942: *The Black Swan*; 1944: *The Lodger; Wilson*; 1947: *Monsieur Verdoux; Unconquered.*

Barry Shipman (February 24, 1912–August 12, 1994)

Writer, co-wrote *Flash Gordon Conquers the Universe.* Active from 1936.

1937: *Dick Tracy* (serial); *The Painted Stallion* (serial); *Zorro Rides Again* (serial); 1938: *The Lone Ranger* (serial); *The Fighting Devil Dogs* (serial); *Dick Tracy Returns* (serial); 1939: *The Lone Ranger Rides Again* (serial); *Daredevils of the Red Circle* (serial); *Dick Tracy's G-Men*; 1940: *Flash Gordon Conquers the Universe* (serial).

William A. Sickner (December 23, 1890–September 18, 1967)

Cinematographer, co-photographed *Flash Gordon Conquers the Universe.* Active from 1934.

1934: *Tailspin Tommy* (serial); 1935: *Tailspin Tommy in the Great Air Mystery* (serial); *Stormy*; 1939: *The Phantom Creeps* (serial); 1940: *The Green Hornet* (serial); *Flash Gordon Conquers the Universe*

Zarkov radios important news in *Flash Gordon*, chapter 10. From left: Frank Shannon, Jean Rogers, Buster Crabbe.

(serial); 1942: *Gang Busters* (serial); 1943: *The Adventures of Smilin' Jack* (serial); 1944: *The Mummy's Ghost*; 1946: *Behind the Mask*; 1948: *The Shanghai Chest*; *The Feathered Serpent*; 1949: *Bomba, the Jungle Boy.*

Frederick Stephani (June 13, 1903–October 31, 1962)

Producer-director-writer, directed and co-wrote *Flash Gordon*. Active from 1930.

1931: *Dracula* (treatment); 1934: *Fifteen Wives* (wrote); 1936: *Flash Gordon* (serial, wrote and directed); 1937: *Beg, Borrow or Steal* (produced); 1938: *Love Is a Headache* (produced); 1939: *Fast and Loose* (produced); *Fast and Furious* (produced); 1942: *Tarzan's New York Adventure* (produced); 1947: *It Happened on 5th Avenue* (co-wrote, Academy Award nomination); 1949: *Johnny Holiday* (produced and wrote); 1953: *Fort Algiers* (wrote); 1955: *Reluctant Bride* (wrote); 1960: *Bomben auf Monte Carlo* (wrote).

Glenn Strange (August 16, 1899–Sept 20, 1973)

Actor, the "Gocko," the "Fire Monster," and two of Ming's soldiers in *Flash Gordon*. Onscreen from 1930. A solid fixture in scores of low-budget westerns, Glenn Strange was also one of the screen's most memorable incarnations of the Frankenstein Monster.

1932: *The Hurricane Express* (serial); 1934: *The Star Packer*; 1936: *Flash Gordon* (serial); 1942:

The Mad Monster; *The Mummy's Tomb*; 1943: *Haunted Ranch*; *The Black Raven*; 1944: *The Monster Maker*; *House of Frankenstein*; 1945: *House of Dracula*; 1948: *Abbott & Costello Meet Frankenstein*; *Red River*; 1949: *Master Minds*.

TV series: *Gunsmoke* (1961–73).

Ray Taylor (December 1, 1888–February 15, 1952)

Director, co-directed *Flash Gordon* (uncredited) and *Flash Gordon Conquers the Universe*. Active from 1926.

1933: *Gordon of Ghost City* (serial); 1934: *The Return of Chandu* (serial); *The Perils of Pauline* (serial); 1935: *Tailspin Tommy in the Great Air Mystery* (serial); 1936: *Flash Gordon* (serial); 1937: *Dick Tracy* (serial); *The Painted Stallion* (serial); 1938: *The Spider's Web* (serial); 1940: *The Green Hornet* (serial); *Flash Gordon Conquers the Universe* (serial); 1943: *The Adventures of Smilin' Jack* (serial); 1945: *Jungle Queen* (serial); 1946: *Lost City of the Jungle* (serial).

Ray Trampe

Writer, co-wrote *Flash Gordon's Trip to Mars*. Active from 1935.

1935: *The Adventures of Rex and Rinty* (serial); *The Fighting Marines* (serial); 1936: *Ace Drummond* (serial); 1937: *Wild West Days* (serial); *Radio Patrol* (serial); *Tim Tyler's Luck* (serial); 1938: *Flash Gordon's Trip to Mars* (serial); *Red Barry* (serial); 1939: *Buck Rogers* (serial); *Boys' Reformatory*.

Richard Tucker (June 4, 1884–December 5, 1942)

Actor, "Professor Gordon" in *Flash Gordon*. Onscreen from 1911.

1927: *Wings*; *The Desired Woman*; *The Jazz Singer*; 1930: *The Benson Murder Case*; *Manslaughter*; *The Bat Whispers*; 1931: *Inspiration*; *The Black Camel*; *Graft*; 1932: *The Shadow of the Eagle* (serial); *Pack Up Your Troubles*; 1934: *The Countess of Monte Cristo*; *The Girl from Missouri*; 1935: *Dante's Inferno*; 1936: *The Great Ziegfeld*; *Flash Gordon* (serial); *Libeled Lady*; 1937: *Shall We Dance*; *I Cover the War*; 1938: *The Girl of the Golden West*; *Test Pilot*; 1939: *The Great Victor Herbert*; 1940: *Road to Singapore*.

Anthony Warde (November 4, 1908–January 8, 1975)

Actor, "Mighty Toran," the forest monarch, in *Flash Gordon's Trip to Mars*. Onscreen from 1937.

1937: *Tim Tyler's Luck* (serial); 1938: *Flash Gordon's Trip to Mars* (serial); *The Saint in New York*; *Marie Antoinette*; *The Affairs of Annabel*; 1939: *Buck Rogers* (serial); *Mr. Moto Takes a Vacation*; 1940: *The Green Archer* (serial); 1941: *Dick Tracy vs. Crime, Inc.*; 1942: *Pittsburgh*; 1943: *Batman* (serial); *Captive Wild Woman*; *The Masked Marvel* (serial); *The Phantom* (serial); 1944: *Charlie Chan in the Chinese Cat*; *The Mummy's Ghost*; *The Thin Man Goes Home*; 1945: *The Monster and the Ape* (serial); *The Purple Monster Strikes* (serial); 1946: *The Mask of Diijon*; 1947: *The Black Widow* (serial); 1950: *Congo Bill* (serial); 1951: *Storm Warning*; 1953: *Houdini*; *The War of the Worlds*; 1954: *Casanova's Big Night*; *Rear Window*; 1959: *Inside the Mafia*; 1964: *The Carpetbaggers*.

Duke York, Jr. (October 17, 1908–January 24, 1952)

Actor, "King Kala" in *Flash Gordon*. Onscreen from 1933, Duke York, Jr. made a specialty of "thug" roles.

1933: *Island of Lost Souls*; *Footlight Parade*; *I'm No Angel*; *Roman Scandals*; 1934: *The Old Fashioned Way*; 1936: *Flash Gordon* (serial); *Fury*; *Libeled Lady*; 1938: *The Spider's Web* (serial); *Topper*

Takes a Trip; 1939: *Navy Secrets*; *You Can't Cheat an Honest Man*; *Union Pacific*; *Destry Rides Again*; 1940: *Nutty but Nice* (short); *The Green Archer* (serial); 1941: *Topper Returns*; *Never Give a Sucker an Even Break*; *Shadow of the Thin Man*; 1942: *Saboteur*; *Invisible Agent*; *Arabian Nights*; 1943: *Three Little Twirps* (short); *Crazy House*; 1944: *The Contender*; *Idle Roomers* (short); *Lost in a Harem*; 1947: *Road to Rio*; 1948: *Shivering Sherlocks* (short); *A Southern Yankee*; *The Paleface*; 1950: *Francis*; *Winchester '73*; 1952: *Confidence Girl.*

Appendix III:
Flash Gordon Remakes

Flash Gordon (1954)

Syndicated television series; 39 episodes (30 minutes each).

Intercontinental Television Films Corporation/Motion Pictures for Television (MPTV); Dumont Television Network (original broadcast).

SERIES PRODUCTION CREDITS

Producers: Wenzel Ludecke, Edward Gruskin; *Directors:* Gunther von Fritsch, Joseph Zigman, Wallace Worsley, Jr.; *Writers:* Bruce Elliot, Earl Markham, Edward Gruskin, Bruce Geller; *Photography:* Arndt Rautenfeld, Jean Isnard; *Film Editors:* Heinz Haber, Roger Pacaut; *Art Director:* Raymond Gabutti; *Set Decorations:* Helmut Nentwig, Raymond Gabutti; *Art Department:* Helmut Nentwig, Louis Boussaroque; *Sound:* Willy Szdui, Jean Bertrand, Paul Durand, Guy Villette, Loiseau; *Special Effects:* F. W. Wintzer; *Make-up:* Igor Keldich; *Camera Operators:* Herbert Korner, Arndt Rautenfeld, Rene Guissart, Jr., Alex Dulac; *Production Managers:* Ernst Liepelt, Jorg Zorer, Rene Noel, Fred Surin; *2nd Unit Director:* Alain Jessua; *Production Consultant:* Joseph Zigman; *Assistant Editor:* Marie-Louise Barberot; *Technical Director:* Louise Grospierre; *Dialogue Director:* Sipora Van Praag; *Music:* Kurt Heuser, Roger-Roger; *Administrative Director:* Maurice Dualt; *Production Secretary:* Eva Ebner; *Script Girl:* Ginette Doynel; *Driver:* Gunther Kortwich.

CAST

Steve Holland (*Flash Gordon*); Irene Champlin (*Dale Arden*); Joseph Nash (*Dr. Hans Zarkov*); Henry Beckman (*Commander Paul Richards*).

Comments

Cheaply produced in West Germany, the short-lived *Flash Gordon* TV series of 1954–55 was a third-rate misfire in almost every department. These shows are so impoverished that they make even the most threadbare episode of the original serials look like *Gone with the Wind* by comparison. Lack of production assets and financial resources aside, the series was all wrong conceptually as well. For some reason, the series is set in the distant *future* (which Raymond's original strip and the Universal serials never were), and Flash Gordon himself, like all TV heroes, has been re-imagined as a cop — he now works for "the Galaxy Bureau of Investigation."

As Flash, Steve Holland (who later served as the model for the *Doc Savage* paperback covers painted by James Bama) is adequate, but Joseph Nash lacks Frank Shannon's moral authority as Zarkov, and Irene Champlin is far too mature as Dale.

For the record, it was this series that was responsible for the extraneous *Space Soldiers* title being attached to the Buster Crabbe serials in order to differentiate the two; both the TV show and the serials were distributed by Motion Pictures for Television at the time.

Flash Gordon (1980)

Universal Pictures/DEG; Released December 5, 1980.

CREDITS

Producers: Dino De Laurentiis, Bernie Williams; *Director:* Mike Hodges; *Screenplay:* Lorenzo Semple, Jr. (adaptation by Michael Allin); *Cinematography:* Gil Taylor (Technicolor, 2.20: 1 aspect ratio); *Production Design/Costume Design/Set Decoration:* Danilo Donati; *Film Editor:* Malcolm Cooke; *Music:* Queen, Howard Blake; *Make-up:* Massimo De Rossi, Mario Di Salvio, Richard Mills, Jane Royle; *Hair Stylists:* Giusy Bovino, Betty Glasow; *Production Managers:* David Anderson, Clifton Brandon, Alexander De Grunwald; *Supervising Art Director:* John Graysmark; *Art Department:* Tom Adams, Count Ul De Rico (*artists — skies and clouds*), Ted Mitchell (*scenic artist*); Emanuela Alteri, Mentor Huebner, Giovanni Lombardo (*production illustrators*); Andy Andrews, Jack Towns (*props*); Martin Bower, Christine Overs, Bill Pearson, Don Sargent (*model makers*); Ted Clements, Ken Court, John Penner, Giorgio Postiglione, Tony Reading, Steve Spence (*assistant art directors*); Galliano Donati, Giulio Tamassy, Peter Voysey, Keith Short, Arthur Healey (*sculptors*); Dennis Murray (*plasterer*); Len Furey, Tony Graysmark, Aldo Puccini (*construction managers*); Vic Simpson (*construction supervisor*); Dennis Griffin (*production buyer*); *Special Effects:* George Gibbs, Garth Innis Frank Van der Veer (*supervisors*); Derek Botell (*flying effects*); Chris Kelly (*special effects editor*); Barry Nolan, Pierre Tilley, David Watson, Michael White (*special effects assistants*); Glen Robinson (*special effects consultant*); Richard Conway (*special effects — models and skies*); John Sorenson (*miniatures*); Norman Dorme (*models*); Ray Monahan, Hugh Wade (*optical cameramen*); Lyn Gerry, Ralph Gordon, Dick Ramirez, Rick Rothbart (*optical technicians*); Louis Lichtenfield, Robert Scifo (*matte painters*); Greg Van der Veer (*blue screen composites*); *Camera Operators:* Roy Ford, Gordon Hayman, David Litchfield, Geoff Mulligan; *Camera Department:* David Budd, Terry Pearce, Peter Taylor (*focus pullers*); Harry Oakes (*skies and clouds photography*); Harry Waxman (*additional photography*); Bob Penn (*stills*); *Electrical Department:* Maurice Gillett (*supervising electrician*); Mickey Wilson (*gaffer*); Carlos Melville, Jimmy Worley (*electricians*); *Sound Department:* Jonathan Bates (*sound editor*); Ivan Sharrock (*sound mixer*); Robin O'Donoghue, Gerry Humphries (*dubbing mixers*); Ian Fuller (*dialogue editor*); Michael Crouch (*footsteps editor*); Ken Weston, Don Banks (*microphone boom operators*); Alan Douglas, John Richards, Eric Tomlinson (*music recordists*); Robin Clarke (*music editor*); John Iles (*Dolby stereo sound consultant*); *Assistant Directors:* Brian Cook, William Kronick, Terry Needham, Michael Stevenson; *Costumes:* Franco Antonelli, David Perry, Julian Gilbert, Giampietro Grassi, Michael Jones, Bruno Lenzi, Riccarda Pierconti, David Terry; *Wardrobe:* Janet Tebrooke (*wardrobe mistress*), Ron Beck, Rene Heimers, Keith Morton, Patrick Wheatley; *Additional Production Crew:* Gordon Arnell, June Bloom (*publicists*); Len Barnard, Mary Breen-Farrelly (*accountants*); Howard Blake (*music arranger*); Diana Bull, Jerry Cormier(*administrative assistants*); Rita Burgess, Michael Greenleaf, David Hitchcock, Jeremy Hume (*assistant editors*); John Burgess, Barbara Markham (*drama/ dialogue coaches*); Denis Postle (*2nd unit director*); Richard Greenberg (*title design*);

Derek Trigg (*assistant editor*); Josephine Knowles, Sandy Molloy, Gloria Offenheim (*production assistants*); June Randall (*script supervisor*); Michael McLean, Mary Selway (*casting*); Bill Hobbs (*coordinator, action and movement*); Bill Lindemann (*laboratory coordinator*); Charles Lippincott (*marketing director*); Gerald Makein (*transportation captain*). Released in both 70mm (6-track stereo) and 35mm (Dolby system) formats.
Running time: 111 minutes.

CAST

Sam J. Jones (*Flash Gordon*); Melody Anderson (*Dale Arden*); Max von Sydow (*Emperor Ming*); Topol (*Dr. Hans Zarkov*); Ornella Muti (*Princess Aura*); Timothy Dalton (*Prince Barin*); Brian Blessed (*Vultan*); Peter Wyngarde (*Klytus*); Mariangelo Melato (*Kala*); John Osborne (*Arborian Priest*); Richard O'Brien (*Fico*); John Hallam (*Luro*); Philip Stone (*Zogi*); Suzanne Danielle (*serving girl*); William Hootkins (*Munson*); Bobby Brown (*Hedonia*); Ted Carroll (*Biro*); Adrienne Kronenberg (*Vultan's daughter*); Stanley Lebor (*doctor*); John Morton, Burnell Tucker (*airplane pilots*); Robbie Coltrane (*man at airfield*); Peter Duncan (*young treeman*); Ken Sicklen (*treeman*); Tessa (*hawkwoman*); Venetia Spicer (*hawkwoman*); Francis Mulligan (*wounded hawkman*); Oliver MacGreevy, John Hollis (*Klytus observers*); Paul Bentall (*Klytus' pilot*); Leon Greene (*battle control room colonel*); Graham Crowther (*battle room controller*); Tony Scannell (*Ming's officer*); David Neal (*Ming's Air Force captain*); Bogdan Kominowski (*Ming's Air Force lieutenant*); George Harris (*Thun*); Colin Taylor (*King of Frigia*); Doretta Dinkley (*Queen of Frigia*); Sally Nicholson (*Queen of Azuria*); Michelle Midwater, Marie Green, Imogen Claire, Kay Zimmerman, Frederick Warder, Stephen Brigden, Lionel Guyett, Ken Robertson (*special movement*); Andy Bradford, Bertram Adams, Terry Forestal, Mike Potter, John Sullivan, Eddie Stacey, John Lees, Roy Scammell (*hawkmen*); Kathy Marquis, Sophie, Kathy September, Glenna Forster-Jones (*sandmoon girls*); Roseanne Romine, Sneh, Magda, Shaka, Lindy, Viva, Beverly Andrews, Frances Ward, Kerry-Lou Baylis, Camella (*Cytherian girls*); Miranda Riley (*Frigian girl*); Lorraine Paul, Carolyn Evans, Tina Thomas, Ruthie Barnett (*Aquarian girls*); Joe Iles, Trevor Ward, Alva Shelley, Nick Abraham, Leonard Hay, Glen Whittler (*Ardentian men*); Jamalia, Jill Lamb, Sunanka, Karen Johnson, Gina, Racquel, Fai (*girls in Ming's bedchamber*); Malcolm Dixon, Tiny Ross, Mike Edmonds, John Ghavan, Rusty Goffe, Richard Jones, Mike Cottrell, Peter Burroughs, John Lummiss, Kenny Baker (*dwarves*); Robert Goody, Daniel Venn, Peter St. James, Steven Payne, Max Alford, Stephen Calcutt, Anthony Olivier, Jim Carter, Stuart Blake, Nigel Jeffcoat (*Azurian men*); Chris Webb, Les Crawford, Peter Brace, Terry Richards, John Gallant, Eddie Powell (*Ming's brutes*); Sean Barry-Weske (*rabbi*); Kevin Hudson (*hawkman*); Derek Lyons (*Arborian priest*); Richard Bonehill (*extra*); *Stunts:* Vic Armstrong, Graeme Crowther, Kevin Hudson, Joe Powell, Nosher Powell, Deep Roy.

Synopsis

Pro-football player Flash Gordon, a quarterback for the New York Jets, and his companion Dale Arden, a travel agent, are in a passenger plane when it is forced down by violent weatherstorms that are sweeping the Earth. They meet Dr. Hans Zarkov, who has learned that the moon is being pulled out of its orbit by a man-made force, and intends to investigate in his spaceship. Zarkov's assistant, Munson, has turned coward and fled, so Zarkov compels Flash and Dale to accompany him on his perilous journey.

Flying to the planet Mongo, they land and are immediately captured by minions of Emperor Ming, the planet's ruler. Ming is immediately attracted to Dale, who is held prisoner in the Emperor's palace, awaiting his pleasure. When Flash protests, he battles Ming's guards but is defeated. Ming orders his execution by lethal gas.

Apparently dead, Flash is revived by Ming's sultry daughter Aura, who, desiring the Earthman for herself, helps him escape. Discovering that Mongo is a feudal police state inhabited by various warring factions, Flash eventually forms a powerful alliance with Prince Barin, the strong-willed ruler of Arboria, and King Vultan, who rules the winged hawkmen from a city suspended in the sky by anti-gravity beams. He leads these allies and the various other inhabitants of Mongo in open revolt against the dictatorial rule of Ming, who is finally overthrown and impaled on the nose of a spaceship when Flash crashes it through the palace, arriving just in time to rescue Dale and free Zarkov.

Comments

With the huge success of *Star Wars* in the spring of 1977, a new theatrical version of *Flash Gordon* was inevitable, and finally appeared in late 1980. George Lucas himself had originally wanted to produce such a film, but was forced to reinvent the project as *Star Wars* when he was unable to obtain the rights to *Flash Gordon*. Whatever the results of a Lucas-produced *Flash Gordon* might have been, the resulting film would at least have been a sincere effort made by a filmmaker who understood the source material; such is not the case with the movie eventually produced by Dino De Laurentiis.

A crass, tasteless and insensitive producer, De Laurentiis has nevertheless been responsible for some good, and even classic, films (*The Shootist*), as well as enjoyable commercial efforts like *Barbarella* and *Danger: Diabolik*. But he has also been responsible for unforgivable duds like the 1976 remake of *King Kong* (surely one of the most despised remakes of all time), which featured an extremely cute Jessica Lange in her screen debut, but little else of value.

De Laurentiis' main flaw seems to be his constant production meddling. His remake of *Flash Gordon* could have been much better; the film was originally scripted by Sam Peeples, a film aficionado who was a fan of the Raymond strip and the Buster Crabbe serials, and who based his screenplay on those sources. The Peeples script was too honest and straightforward for De Laurentiis, however; he threw it out (this script was later used for an above-average *Flash Gordon* TV cartoon series and movie produced by Filmation) and handed the writing chores to Lorenzo Semple, Jr., who had been primarily responsible for the deadly campiness of the *King Kong* remake and (earlier) Adam West *Batman* TV series and feature film. The results were inevitable; *Flash Gordon* emerged as a jokey spoof contemptuous of its source, a vulgar, heavy-handed put-on that never realized the potential of Raymond's original material.

Still, the 1980 *Flash Gordon* isn't *all* bad — or at least isn't nearly as bad as it might have been. Ignoring the incompetent lead (a wooden, miscast and dramatically inept Sam J. Jones), the *casting* is good. The two female leads (Melody Anderson as Dale and Ornella Muti as Aura) are beautiful, with Anderson recalling Jean Rogers and Muti looking somewhat more exotic than Priscilla Lawson. Max von Sydow is excellent as Ming, basing his performance (as he admitted in published interviews) on Charles Middleton's original interpretation of the character.

The sweeping production design, although the onscreen results seem to fall short of the movie's publicized $30 million-dollar budget, at least partially realizes the epic nature of the material; and even the rushed, unconvincing special effects seem to echo the visuals of the Universal serials. Also, the bright, sharp, widescreen Technicolor photography, bold and lurid, is a definite asset (the British release prints, struck at superior labs, were of far better quality than the dingy, grainy prints distributed by Universal in America*). Still, although it is somewhat better than the De Laurentiis–produced *King Kong*, *Flash Gordon*, with its inappropriate music score by the rock group Queen, and its devastatingly bad lead actor, is a major disappointment. Certainly, it would have been far better if the original Peeples script had been filmed, and the movie had been made in an honest, straightforward manner, with a little more taste and sensitivity.

*The print material used for the current DVD release by Universal is far superior to their 1980 theatrical prints.

Index

Numbers in **_bold italics_** indicate pages with photographs.